SUNDAY
BLOODY
SUNDAY

Also by Penelope Gilliatt

NOVELS

One by One
A State of Change
The Cutting Edge
Mortal Matters

SHORT STORIES

Come Back If It Doesn't Get Better
Nobody's Business
Splendid Lives
Quotations from Other Lives
They Sleep Without Dreaming

PLAY

Property

CRITICISM AND PROFILES

Unholy Fools
Three-Quarter Face
Renoir
Jacques Tati

SUNDAY BLOODY SUNDAY

*The Original Screenplay of
the John Schlesinger Film*

*Produced by Joseph Janni
for United Artists*

With an introductory essay,
"Making *Sunday Bloody Sunday*"

BY

PENELOPE GILLIATT

DODD, MEAD & COMPANY
New York

John Schlesinger and Joseph Janni worked
through the later versions of the screenplay with
me and I thank them, as well as the actors
and the crew.

P.G.

Stills from film © 1971, United Artists Corporation.
Provided courtesy of MGM/UA.

Published by Dodd, Mead & Company, Inc.
79 Madison Avenue, New York, N.Y. 10016
Distributed in Canada by
McClelland and Steward Limited, Toronto
Manufactured in the United States of America

Designed by Claire Counihan

First Edition

1   2   3   4   5   6   7   8   9   10

Library of Congress Cataloging-in-Publication Data

Gilliatt, Penelope.
Sunday bloody Sunday.

I. Sunday bloody Sunday (Motion picture) II. Title.
PN1997.S833   1986   791.43'72   85-27455
ISBN 0-396-08492-3
ISBN 0-396-08539-3 (pbk.)

Making *Sunday Bloody Sunday*

A FRIEND OF MINE who had started scrubbing at fourteen and went on to be a barmaid had forty years of film-going behind her by the time I knew her. She went to the flicks in London three times a week, sitting in the cheap seats for a double feature. She knew films backward, and often muttered the lines ahead of the actors when we were watching a revival on television. "That Clark Gable is the most gracious in his talk," she would say. Or "Barbara Stanwyck gives you the tongue of America, doesn't she." Or "Leslie Howard has the mark of a gentleman whenever he talks about music." Or "You know, they sometimes have to do a shot two or three times, dear. I often wonder where they get the time for their writing." There lay the only mistake she ever made: she was quite convinced that actors wrote their own lines. "Sir Laurence Oliver" definitely wrote *Henry V*. Sir Laurence was always "Oliver" and always admired.

Perhaps she was not so far off, for it was seldom in her days that scriptwriters wrote the script. The front office did, the producer, the producer's wife. "An original script," or what is piously called "an original," as in the "hand-done oil paintings" that are sold in bad art shops in London, remains hard to find in American or English film-making. It is said not to be "bankable." A bankable script in the English-speaking cinema is still, by and large, an adaptation of a stage hit or a best-selling novel.

In the late sixties, I was asked to write an original script for John Schlesinger and the man who often produced his films, Joe Janni. The offer came through my indispensable young English agent, Clive Goodwin, when I was film critic of *The Observer* in London.

Clive died only a little later because of Hollywood: after lunching with a producer, he was sick on the red carpet of his Beverly Hills hotel, carted off in a squad car because a desk clerk thought he was drunk, and died of a brain tumor in a night cell. Terrible things are engendered by the panicky amorality of Hollywood; typical that the place with deaths such as Clive's on its hushed-up conscience should have thought that "disaster" films had to be fictionalized.

Clive was a friend and he thought this film offer held something. I said "Yes" to the invitation. We drove to see John on location in Dorset. John was shooting *Far From the Madding Crowd* in an ocean of mud. We had a late dinner, the four of us, in the cottage where Joe and John were temporarily housed. I remember that Joe said, "It's beginning to seem like home." John said firmly, "No, it isn't." I think that he particularly was reminded of public school. Crack-of-dawn rises, mud, long evenings of prep in the form of rushes (dailies). But he and Joe were spirited, considering the vexatious mixture of crisis and delay that is the mark of film-making for the director and any working producer.

John had what he apologized for as the germ of an idea. He expressed it in about three sentences. It happened, for me, to kick off a straight progression from a novel of mine that had lately come out, *A State of Change*. As we talked, the

film would have three principals: like my novel, they became, for me, a professional young woman (Alex), a professional man (Daniel) who John wanted to be Jewish, and a
bisexual go-between called Bob with whom both were in
love. The Pandarus character, as I saw him, was both more
flip and more lost than either of the others found him. The
male lead became a doctor in my head as Clive and I were
driving back to London, more and more oddly a direct ex-
tension of the one I had written about in *A State of Change*. It
had seemed, in Dorset, immediately easy to say "Yes";
daunting, demanding, a rare chance to make a packed and
grown-up film about compromises, piercing break-ups, de-
cisions both impossible and necessary. Neither John nor I
ever really believed that we were embarking on a picture that
would be recognizable to more than two and a half people.

I wrote the full draft in three months. A good three-quar-
ters of that was taken up with note-making and working on
the structure. The energy seemed to me to spring backward
from the end, which I wrote first. The last scene—Daniel
learning Italian by gramophone record, ready for a holiday
with his Bob that will never come to fruition—evolves from
obedient repetitions of the tourist infantilisms droned by the
record to a rebellious speech made straight to camera about
the grown-ups who tell him that he is well rid of Bob. No,
Daniel says to camera, or us: half a loaf is better than no
bread. I wrote the scene on a train in Switzerland. I was
going to see Nabokov to write a piece about him. I knew that
Daniel's decision was going to be the opposite of Alex's
though it has the same effect: she was going to quit her half-
life with Bob rather than settle for short shrift and fake hap-
piness on the run. There was plenty of time to think. It was
a long journey from Montreux to the grand hotel in the

mountains where Nabokov was hunting butterflies. Eight hours, as I remember.

From then on I wrote as usually recommended, from the start. (Though the usual doesn't always work best. E.M. Forster once said something about the importance for a writer of knowing "the weight in the end of the tale." Perhaps he meant "tail." That final speech, which is sitting in front of me now in the original black leather notebook surrounded by notes about Nabokov and his card indexes, was certainly a thrashing fish tail.) Alex and Daniel are deliberately seen against the background of their parents as the film goes on, and they are rootedly English. Bob is parentless as we see him in the film, and a citizen of the mid-Atlantic. His attachments are fugitive, like his here-today pop art. He is on the make because his random world has so far declined to be the making of him. He is as binational as he is bisexual, a charmer without conscience; he provides the other two with fun and lightness, and plagues them with his undependability. His promises are seldom kept, and "duty" is fatuous. The other two remember the Second World War with a vividness that grows as they grow older; he is not a great deal younger, but he thinks that any dwelling on the past is a waste of time. No reader he, no music lover. Hope lies in smash-and-grab chances, in possible first-option contracts, not in yellowing old opera scores. Daniel plays, thematically, "Così fan Tutte," recognizing the grief lying in this unequalled Restoration comedy of music. Alex, like Daniel, views the go-getter present with sad contempt and, being like him again, does something about it. She has a job finding new careers for businessmen made redundant, and she is sick at heart with the way our society throws valuable people on the rubbish heap because they are nearing retirement age. Bob is after S. P. Q. R.: not in the Latin sense, but "small profits, quick returns." The others want things to last; Bob believes in the disposable, in gags and gadgets that can be swiftly marketed.

Glenda Jackson was the obvious choice for Alex. Anyone who had seen her work with Peter Brook at LAMDA, or her Ophelia, could have been in no doubt. I once wrote about her that she was the only Ophelia I had ever seen who was capable of playing Hamlet. Peter Finch, who had worked with John before, played Daniel. I believe it to have been the part of his career. He had to come into rehearsals later, but he made up for lost time at the studios at Bray, wandering around the sound stages with a script in his hand. We had known each other for a long time. He had a reputation as a hell-raiser, but not when he was working. One morning, when he was not on call till the afternoon, we sat on the nibbled-looking grass at Bray Studios and went through the script for the umpteenth time. He wanted to talk about the shifts in style and went through the last scene. He saw that it moved toward techniques now often held to be the theatre's unique prerogative; but in the early days of cinema, in today's France and Japan and anywhere but our hidebound studios, movie-making and movie-acting have been free to draw on any sources they wanted. His training was in the theatre, mostly in the classics, and he leapt to the idea of adding to film-acting's possibilities the stage's right to soliloquies and asides and speeches addressed directly to the audience. He had seen a lot of Godard's work for just that reason. The early directors of cinema used the full vocabulary of theatre and camera technique; why lose it? Peter was a rare actor. He is keenly missed.

The part of Bob was most hard to cast. John and Joe had long since generously cottoned on to the fact that I could be useful to our work in parts of film-making that are often roped off from the writer. Together the three of us had to reject name after name that came up in our minds. In the end I put together a test-scene that was not in the film; to use anything in the script itself always fixes things inflexibly for the chosen actor later. John tested three actors. Two of them were skillful professionals, but they were both without the quality we wanted, a quality of being strange to the established world. The Bob we needed had to seem a being dropped out of nowhere. Our secret vote about the tests was unanimous: for Murray Head, who had been in the London production of *Hair*. Essentially a performer and not, I think, eager to learn to act, he was to give John a lot of directing difficulties, and not all of them technical. One day he turned up with a burn on the side of his nose. He explained cheerfully that his girlfriend had stubbed out a joint the night before on the nose-profile that John and Billy Williams, the cameraman, needed for close-ups. Shooting schedules were thrown into chaos.

Most of the final and shooting scripts were planned and finished at my house in London. It has a drawing-room big enough for three people to roam and ponder, and for any number of people to be seen for casting rehearsals. I worked overnight on my anchor of a typewriter, called portable but denied as that by many a gallant man when I have moved around the world with it and help has been offered at airports. As John and Joe left, work began. Neither of them is a writer. Both, interestingly, found the script to be telling themselves something about themselves. It is biographical or autobiographical about no one, but no writer would find it anything but natural if readers or listeners to fiction found it close to home. A Latin American may find a truth about himself in Dostoevsky. Any decent writer will have letters from anywhere, always moving, saying "How did you know this about me?" We spoke of a lot of extra scenes but nearly all of them were scrapped. Joe has a remarkable sense of structure and contributed a great deal where most producers subtract. When he got excitable he spoke English with such a heavy Italian accent that he sometimes seemed to be speaking Latin. There is one scene where Daniel, hearing that Bob has wangled some extra time for them to be together, says, "What a bonus." Joe spoke for many days about "the bonnus scene" before John or I were sure what he meant. We planned a scene in a sculpture gallery, epitomizing something about Daniel's search for anything that will last, and then junked it. It seemed redundant. John tried to edge out a reference by Peggy Ashcroft as Alex's mother to the General Strike because he said that no one would understand what she was talking about; but in the end, after I had been working on the scene overnight, he read it and said (it was a phrase characteristic of him after some gale of director's worries had blown itself out), "I take your point."

We rehearsed the scene, an end-of-dinner scene, in Dame Peggy's house. She knew her lines from the beginning, and concentrated on experimenting with her moves around the seated Alex, alone with her: when to stand behind her, when to lift the weight off her by some family normality with an after-dinner chocolate. With the precision of this great actress, she found the exactness that was needed. Her attention to Alex, and her confidences, are the character's way of helping her divorced and unhappy daughter to hold herself together. Alex is thinking of quitting the Bob she loves because "There are times when nothing *has* to be better than something." She thinks she is quite alone, and has always believed her parents to be content with each other.

I had given the mother a sudden confidence to Alex that makes her see that she is not alone at all: a shock about a political split between the couple in the Depression that made her mother leave her father for a while. The decision Alex is contemplating suddenly turns out to be in direct line from her mother's own judgment that there are times when decks must be cleared for all it may cost. Dame Peggy asked careful questions about the scene and its context, talked the lines through to herself, minutely rehearsed the moves she found crucial. Her mind—and therefore her diction, which always ends cleanly at a full-stop much as a good Bach performer plays without rubato—brings solitary perplexities into the clear air of older and unsuspected allies' understanding of their own pasts. The scene carried Alex through her ending of a love she cleaves to but knows to be not enough, not enough at all.

We rehearsed in an offshoot of some dingy restaurant near the Tottenham Court Road. John was always ahead of time, like everyone else, apart from the actor we soon replaced with Peter Finch. He is too gifted to name but he was too anxious about this part to play it. He was nervous of it, nervous of John, nervous of the rest of the cast. The car we shared to rehearsal—he picked me up—arrived more and more unpunctually. Alarm clocks hadn't gone off, his housekeeper hadn't woken him. Having to replace an actor is a sorry business all around.

At rehearsal, the actors sat at a table to work on the scenes between principals. John stood behind them, near the continuity girl. The costume designer—Jocelyn Rickards—was off in a corner making piles of clothes that were to be auditioned in one of the never-existing gaps. Glenda had her own look and kept to it. She turned her hair chestnut and was at her best in longish skirts and leather tunics over them. In rehearsing the one-to-one scenes, we would begin without notes, with me crouching beside one or the other actor and listening to the lines. Sometimes I could hear a difficulty for Glenda that she had been brooding about overnight, and with a nod from John we would get up and play the scene through with moves, sometimes improvising an extra line, sometimes cutting. This was the way we worked on the fuse scene. Glenda needs to be on the move when she is thinking out a scene. She has a sense of the whole that is remarkable for an actor. Many actors read only their own lines and have no idea how they will play in context. Glenda sees a scene whole. By working together she saw how to make the energy of the fight that starts in the basement carry her through yell after yell to Bob from floor after floor, leading straight from a flaming spat and her furious ''Perhaps you're spreading yourself too thin'' to her ''Sorry, sorry, sorry, sorry'' in another set, shot close in, arms around him.

Peter, starting later in rehearsal time, never needed a change. He bent himself to the text. With Murray, I could often make things better for him by breaking up a sentence into parts that seemed haphazard in a way characteristic of Bob's temperament, which continually picks things up and puts them down again to go onto something else. His life is a bedroom of emotions abandoned like half-finished socks knitted for some forgotten war.

The main work that can be done on the film-making itself by a writer is during the rehearsal and editing times. It is to John's and Joe's credit that they knew this. They are fine working film-makers both, unlike a lot. A Hollywood producer with loads of Monaco money has just rung me (reverse charge) as I write, to say that he just *loves* my new film script, what is its name, remind me, remind me. Seriousness unflagging, I supplied the name. He said, "I can't hear, it's a terrible line, know what I mean," and then came through hot and strong with "It's wonderful, it's an English surrogate myth for Manhattan, sibling myth, gentle, know what I mean? I'll back it if you'll put in a car crash, hear what I'm saying?" I said that I thought I had, adding "Sorry" for no good reason.

When John was shooting and when I was in America working, he once rang up in desperation and asked for a couple of lines to get a character across a gallery in Alex's studio. It was easily done—ninety seconds—and all credit to John to have rung. He recognizes the sound of an original voice and, being musical, and good enough to believe that he is not a writer himself, he made the transatlantic call. I was soon back, because we were editing. The film was running a good twenty-five minutes longer than it should. From the last rough-cut I saw, it had been obvious that we could shave at least eight minutes out of it. Billy Williams, a great and modest cameraman who typically dislikes the ornate description "cinematographer" that others insist on, shoots with a rare ear for the characters' dialogue and a rare eye for gestures and pauses. Together we found a good many scenes where Glenda had the punch line and didn't need it. Her strength of character and force of expression did it. We would cut the line and keep the camera on her face, with the punch line coming from the unseen character. The way had grown clear in rehearsal: I would slip round to Annie Skinner, the continuity girl, and she would "fix" (make firm) my cuts in the master. Annie is a remarkable woman, trusted by John—not everyone is—and much valued by all of us. John would absently run his fingers through her long blond hair in a pause when we were all thinking. She deserves to

be a producer; people of her calibre are much needed for the
job that is more often characterised by a craven sort of des-
potism.

With the concern about the number of minutes that we
had to cut, I was back in the viewing room. John, Joe, Billy,
and Annie were there, and the editor, Richard Marden. I
looked at John after we had seen the rough-cut and said I
had thought of a possible big section to lose. He made a hap-
less gesture, this usually assured man who likes to wear a
jaunty spotted handkerchief round his throat. I went back
into the projection room, and the editor and I worked over
the Moviola; then I asked him if he'd try cutting from here
to here. The here-to-here was a deliberately prolonged set of
jumped scenes: lapses in the time flinging by as Alex gets
later and later, in shots and time-jumps that stutter about
the forgery ahead. Friends of hers and Bob's ("We should
have feared false friends / When we did feast": *Timon*) have
set up for them them a mock parental weekend to care for
their gang of ruefully liberated children. The friends live in
Hampstead, a well-off left-wing part of London. They, too,
are free spirits with a vengeance. Like many cult leftists, they
are dead keen on convention and feel sure that Alex and Bob
will see the glory of family life and be married by Monday.
Famine relief posters hang in the richly appointed kitchen.
The fridge is full of enlightened foods that no child in its right
mind would touch. The eldest of the children, Lucy, uses as
a moral butler or bodyguard a dog called Kenyatta. The real
mother, well-intentioned and ill-tuned, is having an awk-
ward affair with an African, with such woodland joy that her
husband is not allowed to be wounded.

So, into this situation, Alex and Bob are plunged. The
fakery of it makes them falter about each other all the more.
But I suddenly saw that the faltering is demonstrated the

minute they meet. In the projection booth, we cut a lot of the prelude of endless postponements by Alex, her telephoned apologies about getting later and later. The cuts worked because the well-meant, heedless hoax of the "family weekend" was laid in already. I hope someone will one day find those cut scenes in some flea-market and think the cuts right. Neither John nor Joe nor anyone else could quite believe that a writer would cut her own works so drastically. Of all the overwrought arguments about the *auteur* theory of cinema, this alone makes me believe that there are no arguments: they boil down to the people involved bending to what they see on the screen, which is always subtly different from the script. "To hold in the mind two opposed opinions at once," wrote Dostoevsky, as best it can be translated: in this case, the idea of the script, and the idea of the way it can best be carried out. Both notions carry, and eventually the realization commands the plan. I would never have seen the self-evident scissor-jobs needed if I hadn't been away from the rough-cut for a time. Film-making is intensely interesting for writers if directors and producers are good enough to let them use their heads.

The title. It had always been *Bloody Sunday*, Sunday nearly always being bloody in the minds of English children: the day of stasis; of grown-ups going to sleep after too heavy a lunch; of mothers in hats straight from church cooking roast beef and Yorkshire pudding and roast potatoes and Brussels sprouts; of desperate people come for the weekend afflicted with the same childish fidgety legs as even grown-ups have in other people's houses on Sundays, escaping with the household labradors to "walk off" the lunch; of rows about the quality of the washing-up, done by the children at high speed (no soap; too little soap; too much soap; not enough rinsing, so that great-uncle's glass of port produces bubbly champagne and a soap taste that, to children, is no more disgusting than alcohol).

But *Bloody Sunday* suddenly presented problems. Some young eager beaver working as a researcher at ten dollars an hour went to the New York Public Library and said didn't I know there was a famous Irish Bloody Sunday? Yes, I said, it *is* famous. In England, sped by a Eumenides of innocent knowledgeability, an English researcher paid at five pounds an hour had been to the British Museum and telephoned me in America, where I then was two days later, to say didn't I know about the Russian Bloody Sunday? Yes, I said. But it still wasn't the English bloody Sunday. She agreed, with sweetness, having got the point in the first place herself, but glad of a job. The total bloodiness of Sundays from childhood to death is due, I think, to the enslaving legend we have made for ourselves, with the help of the enslaving Old Testament, that time off is fun and work is at the behest of others. On the contrary, diligence is native to the species, as one only has to watch a three-year-old to know, when it is pottering about on its self-invented projects of collecting stones, or making the sounds it likes on a broken plumbing pipe in the order it likes, or getting the blotting paper out of school ink wells, or numbering books. It is to break no holy rule to pursue things seven days a week. If there is any communal god, apart from the jealous deities that dictators have invented for their own warlike purposes, and if he takes one day in seven off, he or she or it should use it to repair the bungles of inadequate imaginings on the other six. A mischievous and motley lot, these idols that mankind has dreamt up for itself. As the research girls in their different ways agreed, Sundays are bloody indeed. Wars break out on Sundays.

But the word *bloody* continued to worry the American front-office people. To them, *bloody* was still as much of a swear word as it was in Shaw's day. Anyway, they said to England on the transatlantic telephone, the English word was *bleeding*. England waited. The telephone went every now and again from many other parts of the world where cross-collateralized films were being shot. *Apex* was suggested forcefully. So was *Triangle*. So was *Every Day of the Week*.

After a fortnight or so, the telephone went again and a well-known voice with a glottal stop of wealth said, "I've got it. *Sunday Bloody Sunday*." But no comma.

THE PLAYERS

Alex Greville—GLENDA JACKSON

Dr. Daniel Hirsh—PETER FINCH

Bob Elkin—MURRAY HEAD

Mrs. Greville—PEGGY ASHCROFT

Mr. Greville—MAURICE DENHAM

Alva Hodson—VIVIAN PICKLES

Bill Hodson—FRANK WINDSOR

Professor Johns—THOMAS BAPTISTE

Mr. Harding (Businessman)—TONY BRITTON

Daniel's Father—HAROLD GOLDBLATT

Daniel's Mother—HANNAH NORBERT

Middle-aged Patient—RICHARD PEARSON

Woman Patient—JUNE BROWN

Rowing Woman (Daniel's Party)—CAROLINE BLAKISTON

Her Husband (Daniel's Party)—PETER HALLIDAY

Man at Daniel's Party—DOUGLAS LAMBERT

Answering Service Lady—BESSIE LOVE

Aunt Astrid—MARIE BURKE

Tony (Bob's Friend)—RICHARD LONCRAINE

Scotsman—JON FINCH

Alex as a Child—CINDY BURROWS

Lucy Hodson—KIMI TALLMADGE

Timothy Hodson—RUSSELL LEWIS

Tess Hodson—EMMA SCHLESINGER

Baby, John-Stuart Hodson—PATRICK THORNBERRY

THE FILM-MAKERS

Producer	JOSEPH JANNI
Director	JOHN SCHLESINGER
Associate Producer	TEDDY JOSEPH
Screenwriter	PENELOPE GILLIATT
Production Manager	HUGH HARLOW
Location Manager	LEE BOLON
1st Assistant Director	SIMON RELPH
Continuity	ANN SKINNER
Director of Photography	BILLY WILLIAMS
Camera Operator	DAVID HARCOURT
Production Designer	LUCIANA ARRIGHI
Costume Designer	JOCELYN RICKARDS
Art Director	NORMAN DORME
Editor	RICHARD MARDEN
Sound Mixer	SIMON KAYE
Chief Make-up Artist	FREDDY WILLIAMSON
Hairdressing	BETTY GLASOW

IN COLOR

UNITED ARTISTS, Entertainment from Transamerica
Corporation

SUNDAY
BLOODY
SUNDAY

Black screen.

Title in white.

Voices over, continuing for a few seconds while screen stays black. A MIDDLE-AGED MAN PATIENT, earnestly hypochondriacal, and DR. DANIEL HIRSH.

FRIDAY

DANIEL

Tell me if you feel anything?

MAN PATIENT

No.

DANIEL

There?

MAN PATIENT

No.

DANIEL

There?

MAN PATIENT

No. I told you, it's over the other side.

DANIEL

There?

3

MAN PATIENT

No.

DANIEL

There?

MAN PATIENT

Yes, that's it.

DANIEL

I can't feel anything.

MAN PATIENT

Yes. My appendix side.
(thoughtful wince)

Cut to DANIEL's hands on PATIENT's stomach.

Movements.

DANIEL

I think we're fine.

MAN PATIENT

What do you mean, we're fine?

DANIEL

I think we ought to lose a little weight.

MAN PATIENT

Why do doctors say ''we''? As if it were *your* pain.

DANIEL
(begins to move to wash-basin)
Why don't you put your clothes on?

MAN PATIENT motionless.

PULL BACK ON DANIEL HIRSH'S CONSULTING
ROOM IN HIS HOUSE IN PEMBROKE SQUARE.
EVENING. FRIDAY, ABOUT 6:00 P.M.

The title "FRIDAY" appears on the film screen.

DANIEL is a doctor in his early forties. Jewish. Clever, humorous face. He has a system of dispensing stoicism that helps to keep at bay his own difficulties. His consulting room is part of his house, small and pleasant.

Little jade elephants and ivory pigs on his desk. A silver photograph of his mother and father, playing two pianos and laughing, stands on a bookshelf behind him. A geodesic sculpture is visible through the window, set in a pretty walled garden with a rock pool.

DANIEL
(washing his hands)
I think it's just possible you've got colitis. Mild colitis.

PATIENT goes on lying down. DANIEL begins to dry his hands.

MAN PATIENT
Colitis can be very serious.

DANIEL
Look, stop worrying, eh? It may be worry that's hurting you.

5

MAN PATIENT sulks. DANIEL moves from couch to desk, taking off his stethoscope.

> DANIEL
>
> I wish you'd stop reading the "Medical Journal."
>> *(in motion, seen from back)*
>
> Remember the pain you had when you thought you had a brain tumour and it was your bowler hat?

> MAN PATIENT
>> *(haughty, cut to the quick)*
>
> This *does* hurt.

> DANIEL
>
> Yes.
>> *(pause)*
>
> I think perhaps it might be an idea if you went in for a few tests.

> MAN PATIENT
>> *(looking over screen)*
>
> Tests! There's something critical.

> DANIEL
>
> There's *nothing* critical.
>> *(affection. Firmness)* There's no question of that.
>
> *(he means cancer, which he can see in the* PATIENT's *mind)*
> It's just in case there's colitis.

> MAN PATIENT
>
> You're hiding something from me.

6

DANIEL

I'm not hiding anything from you. This is probably
nothing at all—

The buzzer goes. DANIEL picks up the receiver and speaks.
The PATIENT stops dressing, stranded. He still has his shoes
to put on and stands there in his socks.

DANIEL

(to SECRETARY*)*
Ask him to give me a minute.
*(he puts his hand over the receiver and goes on talking to
the* PATIENT*)*
—But I've got to be sure, O.K.?
(pause. Gaze between them. DANIEL *takes his hand off the
receiver and speaks)*
Sorry. Look, I'm with a patient.

The MAN PATIENT sees an advantage to be had from DANIEL'S
intimate voice.

MAN PATIENT

(silky)
Do you want me to leave?

DANIEL

No, of course not. Finish dressing and come over
here.
(into receiver)
Can I ring you back? . . . Well, it shouldn't be long,
but I can't now. Try and stay in for a few minutes,
will you? . . . O.K., but just *stay there* for a few minutes, can't you? Right . . .

7

(after putting receiver down)
Now, how's next week?

MAN PATIENT
I can't next week. I've got to go to Brussels.

DANIEL
All right, then. The one after.

MAN PATIENT
(scared, getting out diary)
I think I'm going to Frankfurt.

DANIEL
Look, which is more important, the pain or Frankfurt?

MAN PATIENT
I came to be examined. Can't you tell by examination, for heaven's sake?

DANIEL
Look, I'm not a fortune teller, you know. I'm only a doctor.

The buzzer goes twice. The PATIENT looks up from his diary.

MAN PATIENT
Again?

DANIEL
It's only Ann to say she's going home. She's putting the telephone through.

8

FRIDAY

MAN PATIENT

It'll be ringing in *here* all the time now.
(he really is rather rattled, and DANIEL *sees it)*

DANIEL

The answering service'll take it.

MAN PATIENT leans forward.

MAN PATIENT

I'd much rather you *told* me.

DANIEL

Listen, old friend. It's not cancer.

MAN PATIENT

How do you know?

DANIEL

I'm telling you.

The telephone goes. Three rings. It stops as the ANSWERING
SERVICE picks up. Then DANIEL picks up and listens for a few
minutes before he puts the receiver down, click.

MAN PATIENT

Someone you didn't want to speak to?

DANIEL

*(standing and handing the prescription to the patient,
grinning at him a bit)*
German measles.

THE OUTSIDE OF DANIEL'S HOUSE IN PEM-
BROKE SQUARE. EARLY EVENING.

London County Council rubbish van. Dustbin business.
Potted bushes for sale are visible at the end of the square,
promising a good summer. Through the folded tennis net in
the middle of the square we see DANIEL opening the door and
shaking the PATIENT's hand. PATIENT walks away.

DANIEL'S KITCHEN. EVENING.

DANIEL has just finished dialling on the telephone. We can
hear the engaged sound. The receiver is on the side of his
head that faces camera, obscuring a lot of his profile (a de-
vice used through the film whenever one of the characters
fails to get through on a call).

DANIEL opens fridge door, finds a bar of chocolate, and starts
to eat.

Detail of telephone exchange transmitting engaged number
electronically.

DANIEL'S WAITING ROOM (IN PRIVATE LIFE, HIS
DINING ROOM). EVENING.

Similar shot of DANIEL's head, hand, and receiver, against a
wall of another colour. Engaged sound on track.

Pull back to show him in room. He puts down the receiver
and starts to turn the waiting room back into his dining
room—piling away copies of *Punch* and *Tatler* into the sideboard, moving candlesticks from the sideboard to the dining
table. An ironically sublime section of "Così fan Tutte,"
used at moments through the film, comes in here.

DANIEL'S WAITING ROOM. EVENING.

DANIEL sits on the edge of a table, dialling the ANSWERING SERVICE.

DANIEL

(on telephone)
It's Dr. Hirsh.

ANSWERING SERVICE

What was the name?

DANIEL

Dr. *Daniel* Hirsh. What were those calls?

ANSWERING SERVICE

I thought I heard you picking up.

DANIEL

Yes, but I didn't take the *numbers*. I had a patient.
(acid)
That's why I didn't speak to them, you see.

ANSWERING SERVICE

Well, there was a call from Dr. Simon; and a call from Mrs. Burke, she says you have the number; and from Mr. Elgin.

DANIEL

Yes. Did Mr. Elkin say how long he'd be in?

ANSWERING SERVICE

He said he was going out straight away.

11

DANIEL

Well, he must have changed his mind. He's still in because it's engaged.

ANSWERING SERVICE

It might be somebody else ringing him.

DANIEL

Look, I do *know* it might be somebody else ringing
him.
    (dignity)
But he needs to speak to me urgently before he goes
away for the weekend, you see. Never mind. Next
time, try to give me his name—

Shot of ANSWERING SERVICE face. Profile and machinery.

DANIEL (voice over)

—roughly right, just this once? It adds a personal
touch. Elkin, not Elgin, and not Alvin either, not All-
cott, not Higgins. You've been taking it long enough,
for Christ's sake—no, I'm going straight out now.

DANIEL'S WAITING ROOM. EVENING.

DANIEL moves chairs into their dining-table position and dials
again on the telephone. It starts to ring.

DANIEL'S IMAGINATION, FILTER SHOT. BOB
ELKIN'S STUDIO PAD. SAME TIME. EARLY EVE-
NING.

BOB is a Londoner of twenty-five who makes a living out of
designing plastic furniture, kinetic sculpture, and various
bits of paraphernalia.

Telephone ringing. BOB going out, ignoring it, putting finger in his TOUCAN's beak. The bell goes on in the empty room. Clutter. Coke bottles, a garden swing-seat used as a sofa, a metal robot seated on a low shelf with work tools and cassettes beside it. Japanese paper lamps, a harmonograph, posters, old socks and sweaters and underclothes. An architect's desk piled with BOB's gadget-making in progress. The calmest thing in the room is the head of a long-horn buffalo on a white wall. The telephone stops. Silence in the room. The TOUCAN jumps up onto the window and looks out.

DANIEL'S IMAGINATION, FILTER SHOT. BOB'S PAD. EVENING.

BOB, sitting alone in his pad, close to the ringing telephone and not answering it. He lights a cigarette.

Close-up of BOB full-face, smoking. (DANIEL's imagination, filter shot.) Ringing telephone sound over.

DANIEL'S CONSULTING ROOM. EVENING.

DANIEL, reaction shot, listening to the ringing sound.

BOB'S PAD. REALITY.

Same time. Totally static view, wide. Telephone ringing in the empty flat, shortly stopping. Then it rings again.

ALEX'S STUDIO. SAME TIME. EVENING.

ALEX is a bright, tender young woman of thirty-four, divorced a couple of years ago. She has a witty face and a habit of peering at people attentively when they talk. It is due slightly to short sight but mostly to great interest. She is startlingly intelligent and though she looks a bit got-down physically, walking with the classic upper-class flamingo

13

gait, she attacks life with exuberance and tough-mindedness when it comes to the crunch, and there is no masochism in her. Her focus on the things she finds absorbing is tranquil and shrewd. All the same, she is fairly far removed from ordinary attention to the practicalities of how to exist, let alone of how to do well. Her areas of abstractedness and her hatred of go-getting people make her job in a business-efficiency firm anomalous, comic, harrowing, and eventually combustible. She has a temperamental dislike of ambition.

This time the ringing on BOB's phone has been hers. ALEX holds on, lying down on her bed with a glass in her hand. Her flat has one big room with a gallery around the top half. There are books up there, and waiting in piles to be put into nearly finished shelves beside her low couch double bed. They are also along one bottom wall and piled on a desk. There are a baby grand piano, and furniture that is a mixture of valuable family pieces and Portobello Road, looking pleasant and absent-minded.

When there is no reply to her call, her calm inexplicably explodes. She is apparently about to scatter like a rocket. She simultaneously bursts off the bed and looks at her watch while she undoes the cap of an aspirin bottle with one hand and pulls the cotton wool out of the top with her teeth. Takes aspirins with water, gagging as she speaks to ANSWERING SERVICE.

ALEX

Oh Christ.

She is a bit pissed, but it is hard to tell. She dials again.

ALEX

Is that the answering service? Look, I'm terribly late.
It's Alex Greville. My watch has stopped. What's the
time?
*(she is putting on her shoes as she talks and changing her
bag)*
If Mr. Elkin rings, tell him I'm on my way and I had
to booze with a client who's had the push . . .
(she upsets ashtray and doesn't pick it up)
I tried to get him, Mr. Elkin, but he's gone already.
Is the traffic bad?

Shot of same ANSWERING SERVICE—profile of head.

ALEX

Yuh; well of course, it would be different round you.
Worse, of course.
(amused)
. . . Like your weather . . . Goodbye.

Sets her watch and throws things into a half-packed grip—
books, jeans, children's books that she takes out of a book-
shop paper bag.

ALEX'S KITCHEN.

Neat. Not at all scruffy. Shelves are in the middle of being
built. She holds her head and makes herself some instant coffee in a hurry, waiting for the tap water to be as hot as possible. The coffee is then too hot to drink and she cools it with
cold tap water.

ALEX'S STUDIO STAIRS.

ALEX runs down the stairs and out of the studio.

The sound of a man singing "I Must Go Down to the Sea Again" floats out into the yard from the studio below AL-EX's. Upright piano accompaniment.

ALEX'S CAR (A TRIUMPH).

Driving to Greenwich through Trafalgar Square and Fleet Street and eventually over Blackfriars Bridge. Impatience. Traffic jams. ALEX keeps looking at her watch.

> OVERHEARD CAR RADIO
> . . . The Chancellor of the Exchequer said today that as long as the present wage explosion continues, the balance of trade must be seriously affected and there will be a considerable threat to foreign exchange rates.

ALEX MEMORY SHOT OF HERSELF ALONE IN HER OFFICE AT NIGHT.

Radio sound over.

> OVERHEARD CAR RADIO
> . . . threatened steel strike. A Treasury spokesman said today that unless the disastrous wage spiral can be halted the purchasing power of the pound will be dramatically affected.

Now ALEX is on the telephone to ALVA HODSON in the HOD-SONS' open-plan kitchen. Both in close-up. ALEX looking troubled.

> ALVA
> You're not bothered about the kids? They like you—

ALEX

—No—

ALVA

It'll be nice for both of you—trust me—

The parent HODSONS, ALVA and BILL, are an agreeable radical couple without much sense of the ridiculous. They think that ALEX and BOB should get married and have kids, and they have asked them to take over their house this weekend to promote the idea. Circular pan around the HODSON kitchen and conservatory, following TIMOTHY HODSON, who is tooting on a recorder. There are four other HODSON OFFSPRING. He skips through them and we see the room as he goes: a mixture of enlightened toys, Victorian furniture, priapic African sculpture, card indexes, and a flagon of cider. The HODSON MONKEY is eating a peanut on a pile of left-wing pamphlets.

ALEX IN A PUB EN ROUTE. CONSECUTIVE TIME, REALITY. TALKING TO LUCY HODSON, AGED NINE.

ALEX is at a coin box in the pub, leaning against the wall. The pub clock says 7:30.

ALEX

Is Bob there?

LUCY

He's a bit furious you're not here yet.

ALEX

Tell him not to be grumpy. Tell him I'm . . . tell

17

Mummy I hope I haven't held her up and I'm hurrying.

White frames.

Clock at 7:55.

Held shot of ALEX leaning against the pub wall for a long time. She can't really hurry. Mysteriously stalled.

Sounds of money on the bar and in the drawer of the cash till.

> FIRST MAN ON BAR STOOL
> *(disgusted)*
> "Disastrous wage spiral." They could afford to pay the railwaymen a decent wage, you'd think. See how much they spend on Prince Charles.

> SECOND MAN ON BAR STOOL
> That's promotion. That's public relations.

> FIRST MAN ON BAR STOOL
> What did we win the war for? They're doing better than we are. Bloody Boches.

> ALEX
> *(to MAN on bar stool in a different voice, submerged, struggling, slow)*
> Is that clock right, do you know?

> SECOND MAN ON BAR STOOL
> Just about.

FIRST MAN ON BAR STOOL

I've got a son emigrated to Canada.

ALEX

Surely it's miles fast, isn't it?

The MAN shrugs. The FIRST MAN is younger, with a black leather motor-bike jacket on.

THE OUTSIDE OF THE HODSONS' HOUSE. NIGHT.

Four of the kids are screaming out of different windows. ALEX drives up in her Triumph behind the HODSONS' station wagon as the HODSONS, PROFESSOR JOHNS, and BOB come out of the lighted doorway and down the path. PROFESSOR JOHNS is a black African sociologist. ALVA, a pretty woman of about thirty-four with an ebullient style and a tired face, does sociological studies with her husband, BILL HODSON. What follows is a background jumble of throw-away apologies and the HODSONS' yelled explanations of humour. Uppermost, intimacy drawing BOB and ALEX together.

ALEX

I'm so sorry—

ALVA

It couldn't matter less, darling—

BILL

It's *better* to arrive there late—

19

BOB
(affectionately)
Two bleeding hours, miss. You're never late. What
happened?

ALEX
I couldn't get started—

Meanwhile, BILL and ALVA are kissing her and she shakes
PROFESSOR JOHNS' hand.

ALEX
(to PROFESSOR JOHNS)
How do you do. I really am terribly sorry.

BILL starts to put cases into the back of the station wagon.
KENYATTA, the HODSON bulldog, runs out to the car and
barges into ALEX violently.

ALVA
(fondly)
Oh, he recognises you. He's glad to see you.

ALVA climbs into the driving seat and PROFESSOR JOHNS gets
in beside her.

ALEX
(to BOB)
They won't be there till midnight.

BOB
(softly)
Well, what's the difference?

20

ALVA and BILL kiss ALEX goodbye from the car.

> BILL

The late Miss Greville.

ALVA laughs immensely at this non-joke and cranes her head through the window to shout at the CHILDREN.

> ALVA

Papa made a joke.

> TIMOTHY
> *(shouting from window)*

What?

> ALVA
> *(shouting louder)*

Papa made a joke.

> LUCY
> *(bawling)*

No, silly, Timothy meant what was the *joke?*

The concentration is now on BOB and ALEX trying to get a bit of privacy among the hubbub. ALEX crosses herself.

> ALEX

What sort of a day did you have otherwise?

> BOB

Better than yours, maybe. There's someone interested in the bubble-tubes.

ALEX

(soft)
Clever you.

ALVA

(overlapping in a yell to LUCY*)*
He said to Alex "The late Miss Greville."

Hilarity from LUCY. Hilarity from the HODSONS. BOB raises his eyebrows. The PROFESSOR smiles, looking at the map.

BOB

(to ALEX*)*
You look a bit tired.

ALEX

I'm fine.

BOB

Bad day?

ALEX

(makes a face)
Busy-busy, not useful-busy.

LUCY

(shouting to the car between laughs)
Oh, well done, Papa. She is *terrifically* late.

ALVA

(bawling to LUCY*)*
Darling, the joke is that she isn't late meaning dead.

FRIDAY

LUCY
(to ALVA, *shouting)*
I already saw that part.

KENYATTA runs again to ALEX and nearly knocks her over.

ALVA
(looking at KENYATTA, *to* ALEX*)*
You know he's eaten already? You know he only has
one meal a day?

ALEX
(patiently)
Two pounds. Two pounds of raw meat tomorrow. I
think I've got it.

ALVA waves goodbye and turns on the ignition.

ALVA
(to ALEX *and the* CHILDREN, *shouting)*
Promise not to let the economic crisis spoil the weekend.

The car doesn't start the first time.

ALVA
(to BOB *and* ALEX*)*
It's worrying about the cost-of-living index, isn't it?
Oh, by the way, John-Stuart's milk is in the fridge.

BILL
(head out of back of station wagon, waving to ALEX *and*
BOB *as car goes off)*
Be a good family.

23

KIDS wave goodbye raucously long after the car is out of ear-shot. ''Così'' starts over next shot.

As the Hodson car drives off, ALVA turns to BILL.

> ALVA
>
> Our old mate the doctor wouldn't turn up unasked, would he?

Long pause after the car has gone. BOB and ALEX hold their positions and then walk to the front door. On the threshold BOB waits. ALEX has her head down, neck forward, hands in pockets. Then she touches his cheek.

> ALEX
>
> What are you thinking?

BOB makes affectionate ''nothing'' reply with his face.

> ALEX
>
> Sure?

HODSONS' BEDROOM. NIGHT.

Start on ALEX coming out of the bathroom door wearing dressing gown over nightdress, brushing her hair. BOB is already in bed watching the Anglican Epilogue on TV.

> CLERGYMAN
> *(on television)*
> . . . and many of you, I know, prefer sports pro-grammes to any others. So do I. We all like to cheer the winning side. But I'm not asking you to come to Christ's side because it's the winning side. Christ

doesn't take sides. He doesn't judge. He cheers for
you as much when you win as when you lose—

BOB turns the sound off. CLERGYMAN continues, silent.

> BOB
> *(improvising for the* CLERGYMAN)
> When I was first following Christ I was terrified he'd
> make me give up football. Now I know you can score
> a goal to the glory of God, or miss it to the glory of
> God.

ALEX crosses to the mirror and looks in it with her back to
BOB. She brushes her hair back.

> BOB
> Don't scrape it.
> *(she turns and looks at him)*
> Come here.

She moves across room, taking off dressing gown and throwing it onto chair, and moves to the far side of the bed in a
nightdress.

> BOB
> *(heavily)*
> What have you got that on for? Take it off.

> ALEX
> *(looking down at it)*
> Yuh, why *have* I got it on?—Maybe because of this
> house, subconsciously. And also because it's so
> bloody cold.

She takes the nightdress off. A rush of white linen across the frame.

ALEX

My god, it's freezing.

TIME-LAPSE SHOTS OF THE HODSON HOUSE AT NIGHT:

CONSERVATORY.

The MONKEY awake.

CHILDREN'S ROOM.

The baby in its cradle.

ANOTHER VIEW OF THE CHILDREN'S ROOM.

The KIDS sprawled asleep.

CORRIDOR.

KENYATTA padding about.

CHILDREN'S ROOM.

LUCY lying awake.

HODSONS' BEDROOM.

BOB and ALEX under the blankets. Movement. A baby cries off-screen. Movement stops and then starts again. ALEX starts to get out of bed.

BOB

If you get up, I'll kill you.

There is a knock at the door.

ALEX

Yes. Who is it?

LUCY

It's me. It's Lucy. Are you awake? Alex? Can you hear? Just to say I'll look after John-Stuart for you.

ALEX

(whispering)
She sounds like someone's mother-in-law. Loitering.

LUCY

(knocks again)
Can you hear? I can hear if you can hear. Alex?

BOB gets out of bed naked, and moves quickly towards the door.

BOB

Come in.

ALEX

(shouts)
No! Stay out! Go away!

LUCY

It's all right. I'll manage.

HODSONS' KITCHEN. NIGHT.

ALEX is wearing a mohair rug from the HODSONS' bed and BOB is in pants and two long thick sweaters. The two of them are eating out of the fridge, which is packed with family food

not looking very eatable. There are large posters about fa-
mine-relief on the wall.

ALEX

(with mild interest)
Do you think Alva and Bill had that disgusting eel and
pumpernickel they gave us? I wonder if they'll be sick
in the middle of the sociologists.

BOB

I want some milk.

ALEX

Milk? I want some wine. You get more and more like
an American.

BOB

What's this?

He picks up a screw-top jar with something milky in it.

ALEX

It looks special. I'll ask Lucy tomorrow.

They sit at the table and eat cheese and bread and tomatoes.
A dog bays.

ALEX

How typical of them to have those posters. In *here*. To
take your appetite away.

BOB

But, well, Alva does that sort of thing.

ALEX

Why the hell did we come?

BOB

Because you're soft.

ALEX

No, because it's a chance of a whole weekend together.
  (eyeing him)
She thinks we ought to get married.

BOB

She's a sort of C.I.A. agent for happy families.
  (eats)
She thinks we're her guinea pigs.

ALEX turns away and opens some wine, then looks back at
BOB and holds his hand.

ALEX

Well, we're not, are we?

LUCY comes in with a heavy sigh, the BULLDOG beside her.

LUCY

You locked Kenyatta out of your bedroom. He sleeps
on the bed.

29

> ALEX

Oh. Well, I *am* sorry.

> LUCY

(graciously)
I don't suppose you meant to.

> ALEX

Is this milk all right for Bob to drink?

> LUCY

It's Mummy's.

> ALEX

Can't she spare it?

> LUCY

It's *Mummy's,* I said, for *John-Stuart.* He isn't *weaned.*

> BOB

Oh my god.

LUCY goes upstairs with the BULLDOG.

HODSONS' BEDROOM. NIGHT. GETTING LIGHTER.

The DOG is asleep on all but the top third of ALEX's side of the bed. ALEX is lying awake. BOB is dead asleep with his head under a pillow. JOHN-STUART cries and ALEX reacts. She slides her bent knees carefully out of the bed, puts on the dressing gown, and goes into the nursery.

LUCY has forestalled her. The CHILD turns the BABY over and copes with rebuking efficiency. ALEX remains on the hover at the door, silent, displaced.

DANIEL'S CONSULTING ROOM. NIGHT. GET-TING LIGHTER.

(Same time as ALEX's.)
We see DANIEL's back bending down to put "Così fan Tutte" on to his complicated Hi-Fi. Close-ups of switches on the mechanism as he puts on the record and starts the music.

DANIEL looks out of his window at the garden, eating from a tube of polo mints.

BOB's geodesic sculpture looms in the garden, looking strange and rather beautiful.

THE OUTSIDE OF DANIEL'S HOUSE. NIGHT.

DANIEL emptying dustbins.

HODSONS' BEDROOM. NIGHT. NEARER DAWN.

"Così" music carries over.

The DOG is still asleep in most of ALEX's place in the bed. ALEX is sitting on the windowsill watching BOB asleep. After a while she kneels on the floor beside him and kisses his hand.

SATURDAY

HODSONS' BEDROOM. MORNING.

"SATURDAY" title on frame.

CHILDREN all over the bed, singing a round, bouncing, reading the "Guardian." TIMOTHY has taken a gulp of ALEX's coffee and he is making a face at it. The BABY is asleep between the DOG's paws.

TIMOTHY

Eech.

ALEX

Serves you right for pinching my breakfast.

Pause. The KIDS look spinsterish.

TIMOTHY

Not *your* breakfast. Papa paid for it.

BOB

There's socialism for you.

TIMOTHY

What does he mean?

CHILDREN crawl over ALEX, smoking. Some of them have chocolate cigarettes, some pot. Indistinguishable.

ALEX
(eyes closed, using a dowager's voice)
It was very nice of you to bring the tray up.

TIMOTHY

Why has she gone old?

BOB

She does it sometimes for fun in the mornings.

LUCY
(to ALEX*)*
Mummy said you'd like a lie-in together in peace.

BOB

Did she mention you coming in with the tray? And staying?

LUCY

We always come in here first thing.
(pause)
Then we watch Mummy and Papa have a bath together.

33

ALEX screams.

> BOB
>
> *(to* LUCY*)*
> Be a good chap and piss off, will you?

> LUCY
>
> *(laughs heartily)*
> I'm not a chap, I'm a girl.

ALEX closes her eyes in some anguish, opening them again with another thing to face entirely.

> ALEX
>
> There's the most peculiar smell in here. It's just like pot. Are you children smoking pot?

LUCY is silent. Pause.

> LUCY
>
> *(to Alex)*
> Are you a bourgeoise?

> ALEX
>
> I don't mind, but does Mummy know?
> *(pause)*

> LUCY
>
> Yes. *Well.* They keep it at the back of the records.

> TIMOTHY
>
> Behind "Tristan and Isolde."

                              ALEX
Yes, but does she mind?
        (to BOB *for advice)*
Bob?

                              BOB
        (to ALEX*)*
I don't suppose it matters.

                              ALEX
        (to BOB*)*
No, O.K.
        (to LUCY*)*
Now, about whether I'm a bourgeoise.

                              BOB
        (to LUCY*)*
She has a bourgeois father who's very grand and owns
a lot of banks. O.K., little comrade?

                    FIVE-YEAR-OLD BOY
        (to ALEX*)*
Do you work for a living?

                              ALEX
Yes.

                              LUCY
What as?

                              BOB
        (leaning back on pillows, in a jolly, swift-speaking mood,
        meaning to make ALEX *and himself sound as stupid to the*

KIDS *as possible)*
She's a business-efficiency expert and I design plastic rubbish. So there you are, mate.

Most of the CHILDREN kill themselves with laughter. ALEX lights a Kent.

LUCY
(to TIMOTHY, *who is still giggling)*
Timothy, stop laughing, he *meant* it.

ALEX
Go away and freak out or something, can't you? And give me your nice liberal newspaper, Lucy. Is this the only one they get?

LUCY
Mummy and Papa read *all* the papers. This is the one they like in bed.

HODSONS' GARDEN, SEEN THROUGH THE WINDOW BY BOB, AND FROM THE LAWN.

BOB is looking through a prism. JOHN-STUART is in his cot. We see the BABY then through the prism: multiple JOHN-STUARTS.

CHILDREN'S voices over.

ALEX is playing on the lawn with the OLDER CHILDREN and KENYATTA. After a while she looks up at the window. Something on her mind.

HODSONS' OPEN-PLAN GROUND FLOOR.

BOB is sitting at a loom fiddling with some gadget of his own. Preoccupation. ALEX is in the foreground, sitting on the sofa with her legs up, looking at him and thinking. Pause. He looks at his watch.

ALEX

Is it too early for a Bloody Mary?

BOB

You sound very cheery.

ALEX

I came to a decision about ten seconds ago.

BOB

What?

ALEX

(sounding fine)
I'm going to give myself the sack at the office.

BOB

What?

ALEX

Quit. Pack it in. I'm fed up with grooming people to be thrusters.

BOB fiddles with the shuttle of the loom.

ALEX

What's eating you?
(pause. Change of voice. Soft)
Hey.

BOB

Are you doing it because of me?

He moves to the mantlepiece. The shot moves round, and ALEX's head follows BOB. Through the following lines we see only the back of her head, in quarter-profile. We can see BOB's briefcase at the end of the sofa.

ALEX

No, my duck. You turn everything to yourself.

BOB silently rummages in his briefcase. He doesn't particularly like getting near her at this huffy point but he needs the thing. Pause.

ALEX

You're not very chatty, flower.

BOB

I've got to go out for a bit.

Pause.

ALEX

Is that so difficult to say to me?

BOB

I've got to go to town.

ALEX

Look, you want to piss off, right? Only don't tell me you've got to work.

He goes towards the door.

ALEX

Wait—wait—wait. Let me guess. What day of the week is it? Saturday. Saturday. I think you're going to see a certain person whose name begins with—D. Whose name begins with D—*A*.
(cheerful voice)
Am I getting warm?

BOB is looking at his watch and counting her out.

BOB

Time's up.

ALEX

Well, fine. You can give me a ring. No, you won't have time. Anyway, take the car.

He gets near the door and she throws the car keys at him. BOB throws them back and grins at her, in hope of a grin in return.

ALEX

(denying him that)
Have fun with.

Close-up at last on her face when the door has banged behind him. Stricken.

DANIEL'S CONSULTING ROOM. CONSECUTIVE TIME.

He is sitting behind his desk. MIDDLE-AGED WOMAN PATIENT.

PATIENT

It's the dirt he brings home I can't stand.

DANIEL
(picking the words carefully for her)
How long is it since you led a normal married life with him?

The PATIENT looks around his room.

PATIENT

This place is kept nice.

DANIEL waits and then pushes her.

DANIEL

How long is it, though?

PATIENT

I can't complain.

DANIEL

You mean he hasn't been near you for a long time.
   (pause)
Or is it that you haven't wanted him to?

PATIENT

He never interfered with me without call.

DANIEL
   (after pause)
Have you ever thought of leaving him?

40

PATIENT
(in a panic, resisting such a dead-right suggestion)
It'd kill him.
(pause)
We don't divorce, our family.

DANIEL
But has it crossed your mind? Sometimes people sur-
vive better apart. Even after a long time together.

PATIENT
(defensive)
What do you know about it? You're not married, are
you?

DANIEL
No.

PATIENT
Well then.
(pause, sad)
Too late to start again, and that's the pity of it. I like
your little elephants.
(pause)
Do *you* think I should leave him?

DANIEL
It needn't be for good. It needn't be anything defi-
nite. Couldn't you go and stay with friends?

PATIENT
I haven't got any . . . not that sort . . . We never had
time for neighbours. It'd kill him, I tell you. Who'd

41

look after him?

DANIEL picks up one of his elephants.

> PATIENT
>
> It was never that sort of thing between us . . . Not what you're saying . . . nothing physical. He just said to me when he proposed, do you think we'd make a go of it? And I said, when he'd got a decent place to offer me, and there it is.
>   *(pause)*
> We've always been good to one another.

He writes a prescription, and puts the elephant into the prescription envelope.

PEMBROKE SQUARE.

BOB walks towards DANIEL's house, carrying his briefcase.

DANIEL'S HOUSE—THE CONSULTING ROOM, PASSAGE AND FRONT DOOR.

> PATIENT
>
> Did I speak out of turn?

> DANIEL
>
> Oh, no. Let me know about the headaches.

> PATIENT
>
> Thanks very much.
>   *(puts envelope in her handbag)*
> Good of you to see me on a Saturday. A doctor never

rests, though, does he? It must be interesting, seeing people.

(they go out in the hall)

DANIEL

I could do with a holiday.

PATIENT

(she doesn't listen to him)
It's a calling, isn't it?

Unseen by her, BOB opens the front door, using his own key. The corridor gets momentarily brighter with the door opening. He goes into the kitchen, raising eyebrows infinitesimally as DANIEL shows the WOMAN PATIENT out, who is crying.

DANIEL

(shaking her hand at the front door)
Next week. Hold on.

DANIEL'S KITCHEN.

BOB waiting. DANIEL comes in.

DANIEL

(changed voice)
Jesus, I wish they wouldn't all cry.

DANIEL and BOB kiss each other.

DANIEL

I didn't expect to see you this weekend.

43

BOB

You're working and it's Saturday.

DANIEL

She said it was a calling. It always makes me want to
be a house painter.

BOB

Are you all right?

They look at each other. DANIEL starts to move into the passage towards the consulting room, BOB following him.

DANIEL

Christ, I'm flaked. I've had three nervous crackups,
two cases of the pox, two German measles, and a case
of advanced leukaemia, and all on a *Saturday*.

DANIEL'S CONSULTING ROOM.

DANIEL sits at his desk, lying down a bit in the chair, watching BOB move around the room. BOB straightens a picture and
moves some ornaments and opens and closes the door on the
little fridge, which has drugs in it. Then he looks at one of
the paintings on the wall opposite DANIEL.

BOB

So you finally bought it. Possessions, possessions.

DANIEL

They told me it would be an investment.

BOB

It's nice.

BOB walks out into the garden to look at his sculpture.

He presses a switch inside the French doors before he goes out and the sculpture lights up.

DANIEL stands by the billowing curtains, watching.

BOB

How's it bearing up?

DANIEL

Fine. I had it on last night in the rain.

BOB

I think it's the best thing I've ever done. Do you think the Americans will like it?

DANIEL

Yes, I should think they'd eat it. In fact, are you sure they haven't thought of it already?

BOB

(tinkering with the sculpture)
Somebody seems interested. Can you switch it off? Now on! Off!—They keep telephoning from New York . . . Now on . . .
(the sculpture lights up again)
. . . if we could do something like this on a fantastic scale—

45

DANIEL

Would it mean you going there?

BOB

Yuh, but if I went, it wouldn't be for long.

DANIEL's outside phone rings. He makes a face. So does BOB. DANIEL picks up the phone and listens.

DANIEL

Yes.
  (*then to* ANSWERING SERVICE)
No, I'm on the line, Answering.
  (*pause. Listens to a patient*)
He's been taking the pills, has he?

CHILD PATIENT'S MOTHER

Well, he didn't seem to like them, he can hardly swallow, I told you.

DANIEL

But didn't you—

CHILD PATIENT'S MOTHER

  (*cuts in*)
He's running a terrible fever.

DANIEL

That's exactly why I gave you the pills . . . To bring down the *fever*. They'll *do* that—that's what they're *for* . . . Yes, I think I know.

> CHILD PATIENT'S MOTHER
> He's running a terrible fever.

> DANIEL
> But Mrs. Hackett, haven't you—actually—given— *the pills I prescribed?* Why don't you just try that?

> CHILD PATIENT'S MOTHER
> It seemed as if it won't do him any good.

> DANIEL
> And let me know tomorrow morning, *but only if his fever hasn't gone down. Otherwise ring me on Monday,* right?

DANIEL puts down the phone and stalks around.

> BOB
> How do you put up with it?

After a bit DANIEL cools down and sits.

> DANIEL
> Do you want a drink?
>   *(pause)*
> Ice.
>   *(pause)*
> How long have you got?

> BOB
> A while.

DANIEL

Is Alex hating it up there? Is Lucy putting her through
it? Why on earth did you go?

BOB

Because she wanted me to.
  (pause)

BOB gets off the desk.

BOB

Because I wanted to.

DANIEL

How the hell did you get away?

BOB

Because I wanted to see you.

DANIEL

Do you want a drink?

BOB has opened a book of Italian photographs.

BOB

Scotch.

HODSONS' KITCHEN. SAME TIME.

ALEX is crying. Radio on to cheer herself up. She's also been
making fudge. She eats bits of it before it is cool and reads
P. G. Wodehouse with her legs up on the kitchen table.
Burning her fingers. The HODSONS' younger daughter, TESS,

is doing a large-scale jig-saw on the floor. ALEX looks at her struggling with the pieces. She picks up TESS and takes her back to the table to sit on her lap, putting the jig-saw on the table with her other hand. TESS looks round at her remotely, and struggles off her knees to take the jig-saw back to the floor.

LUCY comes in.

> LUCY
>
> I've come to get the fudge.

LUCY looks at the tray, nasty little inspector.

> LUCY
>
> You've *eaten* it.

> ALEX
>
> Well, it was me that wanted it in the first place, me that made it, and there's a ton of it left.

> LUCY
>
> Where's Bob?

> ALEX
>
> Out.

ALEX has another piece, burning her mouth again but pretending not to.

> LUCY
>
> When's he coming back?

ALEX

Soon. What are you all doing?

LUCY

Why don't you know *exactly* when he's coming back?

ALEX

Oh, do stop, lovey. I do know. I just can't be bothered to tell you.

LUCY

Has Bob walked out on you? I expect that's why you're overeating.

DANIEL'S CONSULTING ROOM.

BOB is engrossed in the book of Italian photographs. Pages of Southern Italian and Sicilian religious parades in hoods that look like the Ku Klux Klan. DANIEL comes in and looks over his shoulder.

Details of book and hands turning pages forwards and then backwards to look again at a particular photograph—Italianate devotions, a skull dressed up like a bride, political photographs.

BOB (voice over)

Bludgeoned into feeling something. I can't see being a fanatic, can you?

DANIEL

Not sure.

More pictures. Mussolini era. A child carrying a cross in a

50

charade of Calvary.

> BOB

Do you honestly feel Jewish?

> DANIEL

Not much, I'm afraid.
>> (*pause*)

Except when I was at school. There were eight of us
out of two hundred and fifty.
>> (*pause*)

I like chopped liver.

More pictures. Landscapes, wine, fun.

> BOB

When are we going to Italy?

Pictures of people together having a good time.

> DANIEL

End of the month?

> BOB

Yuh. Could we take the car?

> DANIEL

I don't see why not.

DANIEL'S BEDROOM. LATE AFTERNOON.

DANIEL in bed. Two-shot with BOB coming out of the bedroom door, dressed.

51

Close-up on BOB coming towards DANIEL, taking off his sweater.

Cut to close-up of them in bed. Naked shoulders.

A telephone rings.

Close-up of DANIEL's face.

Cut to his hands switching off the control button of the ringing.

The sound continues faintly from the downstairs telephones.

Close-up of BOB's and DANIEL's faces waiting for the ANSWERING SERVICE to pick up.

Everything stops for answering services.

DANIEL

Three. Four. I told them to pick it up at three. Six. Seven. Ye gods, eight. They're never going to answer it.

Eventually the ringing stops.

TUBE TRAIN. EVENING.

BOB standing propped in a tube reading the "Evening Standard." We see him through a gang of cheery people coming back from football at Tottenham.

Then he gets out through the crowd and makes for his connection back to Greenwich. He stops at a gadgety type-machine and punches out his name two ways in tin. "Bob Elkin." "Elkin."

HODSONS' DRAWING ROOM. NIGHT.

ALEX is sight-reading "The Jolly Farmer" from the kids' piano music. There is a plate of fudge on the side of the piano. After playing for a time she suddenly looks round, aware of someone's eyes on her, and sees the MONKEY sitting in an armchair staring at her, apparently infuriated by the music. She throws a piece of fudge at the animal to send him back into the conservatory. At this point the lights suddenly fuse. She gropes her way towards the door and swears.

HODSONS' PASSAGE.

BOB is back and at the fuse box, up on a ladder. ALEX leans against the opposite wall of the passage, pointing a torch at him in a caustic mood. One light only is still working, outside the back door at the far end of the passage.

> ALEX
>
> Do put the main switch off. You'll electrocute yourself.

She holds the torch up for him.

> BOB
>
> Do you think I don't know how to mend a fuse?

> ALEX
>
> *(factual, affectionate)*
> Yes.

He pulls the main switch off and the light at the far end of the passage is now, of course, dead. ALEX passes him the torch. BOB looks at a fuse and picks it apart. He puts it back, pulls the main switch on, and the light in the passage is still dead. She goes on leaning against the ladder to stop it slipping.

BOB

Why the hell don't we have those American fuses in England?

ALEX

Darling, as soon as you get yourself into a jam you say it's better in America. How do you *know?* You've never been there.

BOB is fiddling with the passage fuse and has managed to make it function again.

ALEX

Well done.

BOB

(irritated)
I'm useless at this.

ALEX

(on edge about the day)
Couldn't matter less.

BOB

Don't push it. Please don't push it.

ALEX

I never mentioned him.

54

BOB
Use his *name* if you can't resist bringing him up.

ALEX
I didn't bring him up.

BOB
No, but I could hear you thinking it.
> *(pause)*

Piss off to the kids' floor and see if anything works up there, will you?

ALEX stomps away, keeping the torch.

BOB
> *(shouts after her)*

Leave me the torch.

ALEX
> *(shouts)*

You can see by the candles.

HODSONS' HALL AND STAIRS. TORCHLIGHT.

Camera follows ALEX upstairs. She is in a flaming spat and bangs her head against the heel of her hand when she gets to the top of the stairs, stamping her feet and swearing. She recovers a bit and starts switching on each one of the row of lights on the landing panel.

HODSONS' BASEMENT. CANDLELIGHT.

Reaction shot of BOB hearing her yelling upstairs.

BOB

(shouting at her)
Does that work?

ALEX

(shouting out of shot)
NO!

HODSONS' HALL AND STAIRS. TORCHLIGHT TO FULL ELECTRIC LIGHT.

BOB

(shouts out of shot)
What about that one?

ALEX

(shouts)
YES!

The lights have suddenly blazed and she is caught as if she were in a photographic flare. The KIDS wake up and yell and the BULLDOG barks. LUCY appears, blinking.

LUCY

Is Bob back? Is everything all right?

ALEX

(going downstairs)
Shouldn't you be asleep?

HODSONS' BASEMENT PASSAGE. CANDLE-LIGHT.

ALEX comes back into the basement. A dusty naked bulb suddenly goes on by BOB's hand as he fiddles with the fuse box.

> BOB
> *(breezy)*
> Eureka. That one can't have gone on since the Crimean War.

> ALEX
> I missed you.

> BOB
> *(what, after all that racket from her?)*
> Upstairs?

> ALEX
> Today.

> BOB
> *(coming down first three steps)*
> Don't go on at me like some possessive *wife*.
> *(comes down the rest of the steps)*

> ALEX
> Well, I *feel* a bit like a possessive wife, after being left alone with five children, one monkey, one dog—

> BOB
> *(overlapping)*
> —you've never complained about it before.

ALEX

Well, I've never been left around before in the middle
of what was supposed to be a proper weekend—

BOB

—you should have said something about it in the first
place.
   (pause)
I know you don't think you're getting enough of me,
but you're getting all there is.

ALEX

Perhaps you shouldn't spread yourself so thin.

BOB

   (walking away)
Oh, drop it.

BATHROOM OFF HODSONS' BEDROOM. NIGHT.

ALEX is crouched on the floor with her elbows on her knees
and her shin in her hands. She looks round and watches BOB
in the shower through the shower panel. He comes out. She
puts her arms out to him and hugs him.

ALEX

Sorry, sorry, sorry, sorry, sorry.

BOB

Silly tart.

Image of his wet back with her hands on it.

DANIEL DRIVING. NIGHT.

Alternating shots of Old London buildings and of neon financial headlines, seen through wind–screen wipers. He draws up at a traffic light. A GLASWEGIAN MAN is standing on a traffic island. He grins into the car. DANIEL looks across at him. The MAN comes over. DANIEL startlingly locks the car doors and waits for the green light. The MAN comes over to him and his face looms into the driving-seat side-window. A COP watches from the other side of the road.

SCOTSMAN

I said hello.

DANIEL turns his head to the steering wheel.

SCOTSMAN

(louder)
You don't remember me.

DANIEL looks round and speaks loudly through the window.

DANIEL

No, I don't.

SCOTSMAN

(shouting)
Look, don't pretend you don't remember me.

The SCOTSMAN bashes the car window with his closed fist.

DANIEL

Stop it!

The SCOTSMAN bashes the car window harder with his fist,

59

and then stops and nurses his knuckles. The POLICEMAN comes over to the car.

SCOTSMAN

Ah, Christ.

DANIEL

(*unlocks car door*)
Well, get in.

SCOTSMAN

(*gets in*)
He'll nab me.

DANIEL quickly examines the hand as the COP comes up. DANIEL winds down his window.

DANIEL

It's all right, officer. I'm a doctor. He's hurt his hand. He thought he knew me. I'll get it bandaged. He didn't see the window was up.

The COP nods reluctantly, sceptical. But DANIEL sounds like a man in command.

DANIEL drives off. He doesn't glance at the MAN.

SCOTSMAN

How've you been keeping?

DANIEL is silent.

SCOTSMAN
My hand hurts. Might be broken.

DANIEL
You're moving the fingers. Bruise, that's all.

SCOTSMAN
(leaning back in car, spreading himself)
Just stop pretending you don't remember.
(pause)

DANIEL
I remember very well indeed.
(he drives coolly and fast)
Actually, you were pissed the *last* time.

SCOTSMAN
Are we going back to your place, then?

The car passes a shop with one of BOB's sculpture gadgets in it.

DANIEL
No, we are *not* going back to my place. I'm dropping you off. And on the way I'm going to the chemist to get some pain–killers for you.

DANIEL starts, unwisely, to overtake a car. Headlights flashing in opposite direction.

SCOTSMAN
Oh, well. For Christ's sake look where you're going. You're not much of a driver. *Doctor.*

61

(pause)
What are you thinking?

DANIEL
(hard voice)
I was thinking about my *brother*. And he's *dead*.
(pause)

SCOTSMAN
Are you in love?

DANIEL
Probably.

He goes past an all–night chemist and parks down a side
road.

SCOTSMAN
(mocking)
Poor old Danny.

DANIEL
Christ, you even remember my name.

The SCOTSMAN winks.

ALL-NIGHT CHEMIST. NIGHT.

Bleached-out and over-exposed. Scene in shades of white.
The usual Saturday night small-hours sight: Indians, Pak-
istanis, junkies, queens. Everything seems a little at a distance, slow and opiate. Emphasis on white overalls and
people too tired, isolated, or in need of a fix to speak. Frigid
pale faces and lips that look cyanose, like clowns'. DANIEL

stands in the queue at the prescription counter. He writes out a prescription on a piece of paper from his wallet while he is waiting. A thin JUNKIE of about seventeen with a prescription for heroin is collapsed with his head on his chest. DANIEL is tough enough, but at this time of night, on this night in particular, he is less inured than usual. A YOUNG WOMAN speaks softly and urgently to another ASSISTANT.

> WOMAN CUSTOMER
>
> . . . Cough pastilles that are safe for a child but very strong. She won't stop coughing. She isn't three, quite. She keeps being sick.

DANIEL meanwhile looks constantly at the BOY getting high in the corner.

> PHARMACIST
>
> *(to* DANIEL, *thinking that* DANIEL *is trying to pick the* BOY *up)*
>
> Yes?

DANIEL hands over the prescription and still eyes the BOY. What he feels is concern, but the PHARMACIST misreads it. It is that sort of night.

> PHARMACIST
>
> *(contemptuously)*
>
> This isn't signed. Could be a forgery. Just an initial.

> DANIEL
>
> *(points)*
>
> That's the way I sign my name. I'm a doctor. Doctors have writing like this.

63

PHARMACIST

You a doctor?

(It *is* that sort of night, certainly.)

DANIEL

I know it's hard to read. H—I—R—S—H.

PHARMACIST

Where did you get this prescription paper?

DANIEL

Look, it's the same signature as my driving licence, isn't it?

The PHARMACIST looks at the driving licence and hands it back sourly. It is unsigned.

DANIEL

Oh. I must have forgotten to sign it. All right, I'll get my instrument case from the car to identify myself. If you're going to be difficult.

PARKING PLACE BY THE CHEMIST.

DANIEL opens his car. The GLASWEGIAN has disappeared from it, with DANIEL's case.

A copy of ''The Lancet'' is on the driving seat. The words ''BETTER LUCK NEXT TIME'' are written across the cover in big capital letters.

SUNDAY

LONDON. NIGHT STREETS.

DANIEL driving his car.

Cut to back-reference shot of multiplying headlights flashing into DANIEL's eyes. The title "SUNDAY" comes up on the screen.

Go to black.

Black screen clears as if hands were coming away from the face.

DANIEL is in bed, hands coming away from his eyes, waking up.

Cut to his hand on window blind, letting light into the shot.

DANIEL comes downstairs, pulling up blinds at various windows and turning off a couple of lights left burning.

THE OUTSIDE OF DANIEL'S HOUSE. SUNDAY MORNING.

65

Closer shot of DANIEL inside the house front door, undoing the chain and fiddling with the double lock. The camera pulls back as he comes out in his dressing gown to pick up the milk and his newspapers. A MAN in white shorts runs by, arms pumping; one of England's frail-looking nuts, tough as nails. DANIEL puts the milk inside the front door and opens the newspapers. He has two copies of the "News of the World."

The door of the next-door house has just opened and CAPTAIN SHACKLETON comes out, also in a dressing gown, with a scarf tucked into the neck. Dapper. He picks up his own newspapers, and DANIEL and he greet each other simultaneously.

> DANIEL
> *(raising voice)*
> Morning.

> CAPTAIN SHACKLETON
> *(raising voice)*
> Morning.

> DANIEL
> I've got two "News of the Worlds." Is one of them yours?

> CAPTAIN SHACKLETON
> *(looking at his bundle)*
> I've got two "Observers."

They exchange newspapers with polite smiles. DANIEL looks congratulatorily at CAPTAIN SHACKLETON's window boxes.

> DANIEL
> Your bulbs are very far on, aren't they?

CAPTAIN SHACKLETON turns away with the "Observer" on

the top of his pile, reading it. We see the muted political headline about the financial crisis. DANIEL turns away with the "News of the World" on the top of his pile. We see a headline about a defrocked vicar.

GREENWICH STREET WITH A VIEW TOWARDS CHURCH IN DISTANCE.

BOB and ALEX with newspapers under their arms are going for a walk with the CHILDREN and the BULLDOG.

LUCY is pushing the pram. There are other PEOPLE in the street—other FAMILIES—with MOTHERS and FATHERS pushing prams. We see, hidden from BOB and ALEX, a small gang of well-dressed CHILDREN with pieces of a broken milk bottle, going along a row of parked cars and scraping the paint with their home-made weapons. A couple of thousand quids'-worth of damage, maybe.

BOB and ALEX pass a WOMAN bending over a pram with a BABY in it, making goo-goo noises at it.

> WOMAN
> How old is he?

> MOTHER
> Three weeks. She's a girl.

> WOMAN
> You can tell, can't you.

GREENWICH OBSERVATORY.

BOB and ALEX are at the telescope. BOB is hogging it. Enlargements of the CHILDREN. TIMOTHY is throwing sticks for KEN-

YATTA. LUCY contemptuously takes over from him and throws the stick far better, as well she may. She wags a finger at KENYATTA and makes him sit on command. Hard discipline. ALEX makes a face. BOB laughs at her.

> ALEX
> *(thankful sigh)*
> Distance.

A GREENWICH HILL. DAY.

LUCY is wheeling the pram again. ALEX and BOB are swinging one of the younger children off the ground on a count of one, two, three. After a couple of times they release the CHILD, who runs around with the others. BOB takes ALEX's hand and LUCY glances at that. The little matchmaker is suddenly jealous, shut out. She abandons the pram and plays hopping games on the pavement. ALEX takes over the pram.

> LUCY
> Look at me.

> BOB
> Yuh.

> LUCY
> *(to BULLDOG)*
> Come on, Kenyatta.

> ALEX
> See if you can beat him up to the next lamp-post.

LUCY and BULLDOG run excitedly, not to the lamp-post but

across the street diagonally.

A lorry turns the corner, jolting uphill.

ALEX

Lucy! Run quick!

The lorry misses LUCY but hits the DOG. No screech of brakes.
Softly over. Moment of impact played on ALEX's face. She
has her hand to her mouth.

Close-up on LUCY's face. A real child suddenly.

LORRY DRIVER
(yelling, climbing out of lorry, frightened)
What the hell do you think you're doing? Letting
children—

BOB

Belt up.

LORRY DRIVER
—arse about all over the road. Lucky for you we
weren't all killed.

BOB
Look, belt up and help, will you? Empty that sack.

The LORRY DRIVER does as he's told.

Close-up on ALEX and BOB bending down over the DOG, with
ALEX's hair swinging over BOB's cheek. He holds the hair
against his face for a second.

ALEX

(low voice to him)
I'll get them home.

She moves the CHILDREN away and walks them home. She looks back and then sees LUCY looking back too. ALEX picks her up and hugs her.

BOB

(shouting to them)
Start a game, and Lucy play my turn until I get there.

Closer shot of the disappearing party. BOB is now in the far distance with the body of the DOG visible beside his feet. He makes the LORRY DRIVER wait with him until the CHILDREN have turned the corner. Then he wraps up the DOG's body in a sack.

HODSONS' KITCHEN.

BOB and the CHILDREN are playing a game of picture consequences at the table. Folding of paper as the CHILDREN draw various heads, bodies, and legs, and then pleasure when they undo the concertinas and inspect the whole figures. LUCY is shaking and tear-stained. BOB is doing well with the kids. There is a chill in the air in spite of the game, and a closing of ranks. ALEX comes in.

ALEX

I've just rung Mummy about Kenyatta. Would it be nice to speak to her?

LUCY

No, we're all right.

But one of the smaller children looks relieved, gets off BOB's knee, and runs to the phone.

Shot of LUCY at the HODSONS' table, drawing something we can't see. Tear-stained. BOB leaning over her.

HODSONS' BATHROOM. SUNDAY, LATE AFTER-NOON.

ALEX is looking for a pill.

> BOB (voice over)
> Alex?

> ALEX
> I thought I'd try going to sleep. I can't find a pill.

BOB is reflected in the bathroom mirror. He comes towards her and takes her in his arms.

> ALEX
> I keep thinking it could have been Lucy.

> BOB
> Well, it wasn't.

He strokes her forehead.

> BOB
> Slow down.

HODSONS' BEDROOM.

Now ALEX is in bed, throwing one leg out of the sheets. BOB is sitting on the floor next to the bed against a couple of pillows. He is looking at her and drawing sometimes on a clip-board. Pre-cue sound of air-raid siren. We go into a se-quence of Consequence drawings muddled up with gas-mask memories. Material of bad dreams.

Filter shot of LUCY running in ALEX's imagination in the Greenwich street—running towards the distant figure of the DOG, without BOB there now.

Memory shot of ALEX at LUCY's age, running down the hundred-yard corridor of her parents' block of flats. The corridor is lined with black-out curtains. She chases out and then down Portland Place, seen from the same angle as the Greenwich street. She is in schoolgirl uniform and carrying her father's gas mask. Her FATHER, in back view, is bicy-cling away down Portland Place: a touching and dignified figure wearing bicycle clips, with a briefcase banging against the handlebars. The London street is full of bicycles. Hardly any traffic. (Petrol rationing.)

Filter shot of heads in gas masks during an imagined gas raid, ALEX's FATHER on his bicycle, without a mask, cough-ing.

Shot of one of the HODSON CHILDREN's completed Conse-quence figures. There is a man's head at the top, a drawing by LUCY of Kenyatta's body and tail, and a drawing by AN-OTHER CHILD of Kenyatta's legs curled up under him. Gro-tesque image, like the heads in gas masks.

> BOB (voice over)
> Can anybody tell me how to draw a boot? I don't seem
> to be any good at feet.

Filter shot of ALEX in schoolgirl uniform, earlier in her recollection, seen in the dining room of what later turns out to be still her parents' home. Breakfast with her FATHER, sitting close together at one end of the table seen later. The air-raid siren goes. MR. GREVILLE gets up and says, "Look after yourself, Alex. I'll do the Latin tonight." Kisses her goodbye. She watches him out of the window, unpadlocking his bicycle from the railings outside. She sees that he has forgotten his gas mask, which is hanging on the back of his chair, and starts running after him. BOB's voice, in reality, follows the recollection of MR. GREVILLE's voice.

> BOB (voice over)
> Lucy, that's a very good middle of a horse.

Shot of another grotesque Consequence assembly with KEN-YATTA's head fixed to the body of a horse and then to a man's trousered legs with big army boots.

Filter shot of ALEX as child running after the now nearly vanished figure of MR. GREVILLE.

> ALEX
> *(as child)*
> Daddy, your gas mask!

He doesn't hear. She grabs a bicycle, but it is padlocked to the railings. She runs after him, panting. Bumping into people. She seizes someone.

> ALEX
> My father's forgotten his gas mask. He'll be gassed.
> *(crying)*
> He'll get killed.

73

The PASSER-BY shrugs and replies in Polish.

HODSONS' BEDROOM. SUNDAY AFTERNOON.

BOB gets up to cover ALEX with the bedclothes. There are close-ups of her beautiful face, intercut with close-ups of BOB's pencil making circling shapes, round and round, like the movement of the harmonograph that we saw in his flat earlier on. The last shot of his doodling melts into the sphere of a telephone dial. BOB telephoning: BOB the not dream-ridden. His memory is shorter than hers and he can always find exits.

> BOB
> *(whispering so as not to wake ALEX)*
> Tommy there?
> *(pause)*
> Hi. Has that thing come back from the workshop yet?
> I still can't think how to hang it. It needs so much
> bleeding room. Look, bring it up, will you? Where I
> told you, yuh.

Go to black. Pause.

Black screen slowly merges into semi-discernible shapes of HODSON bedroom. Much time has passed. ALEX has been right out for a long time. There are faint voices from downstairs and upstairs. The door is ajar. There is a glow from the windows of the houses opposite. She is quite lost for a bit. Where am I, what day?

HODSONS' KITCHEN. EVENING.

ALEX is coming down the stairs. She takes in a scene that looks like the HODSON household just as she has always known it. ALEX usurped. Wide-shot panorama of chaos with ALVA

in imperturbable command of it. Cases and typewriter-lid
unpacked from the car are on the floor. ALVA is cooking at
high speed for unidentified numbers. The MONKEY sits on the
work-tops. The CHILDREN are at one end of the table finishing their supper, supervised by LUCY. PROFESSOR JOHNS types
at the other end of the table. TIMOTHY has left his place and
is banging a tambourine and an African bongo drum around
PROFESSOR JOHNS. ALVA is shouting at the CHILDREN to get
them to bed.

ALVA

Bed—bed—bed! Timothy, stop it! Come on, bed!

CHILDREN

Not yet, Mummy! No! Not sleepy!

ALEX has entered.

ALEX

I'm so sorry. I must have been flat out for hours.

ALVA

We crept up but you looked as if you needed the rest.
    (to children)
Come on, bed! Timothy, bed!
    (Timothy is banging even louder around PROFESSOR
    JOHNS)
Stop banging! Come on, say goodnight to Alex.

ALEX bends to kiss CHILDREN. The SMALL CHILDREN go, under LUCY's charge.

ALEX

(to ALVA)
I'm so sorry about Kenyatta.

ALVA

It must have been awful for you.

ALEX

For *us?*

Pause.

ALEX

Where's Bob?

ALVA

(stiffly)
He's upstairs with his mates.
Working. In the middle of your weekend.

ALEX looks apologetic.

HODSONS' PLAYROOM.

TONY and his girl, RENEE, are sitting on a climbing tree.
TOMMY is talking to BOB. PIP, TOMMY's girl, is parked in an
armchair with a tonic water. RENEE and PIP are the true con-
temporary birds. Silent, long-haired, groomed, beautiful,
and entirely without expression. They might be impassive,
or simply bored. The harmonograph is being gently handed
from BOB to TOMMY while they talk about how to suspend it.
ALEX is sitting on a rocking-horse close to BOB: an old merry-
go-round horse, with her hanging onto the stem.

BOB

Yuh, O.K., that's beautiful, but we've still got to work out how to hang it.

BOB holds up the harmonograph so that it starts to make drawings.

TONY

Still can't see why it can't be on adjustable legs.

BOB

(*to* ALEX)

Look, suppose you were an American businessman. Would you sooner it was on adjustable legs where anyone might bash into it but where you could move it, or would you sooner it was on the wall?

ALEX holds up the harmonograph, first free-standing, and then against the wall.

ALEX

(*choosing the wall*)

Like this.

(*to* BOB)

It's worked, hasn't it?

(*very pleased—with him. Shit* ALVA's *piety*)

Tommy, anything against it?

BOB

He's found there'd be some manufacturing problems but I've always thought we'd do better to sell this one outright. You know English delivery dates.

77

TONY

(from climbing tree)
If I were an executive, I'd want it on the wall.

TOMMY

It'll be the New York equivalent of worry beads.

Shot of harmonograph quietly making spirals. Tommy's voice continues over.

Executives don't like playing with pens all their lives. This is calming. That's why they like fooling around with lawn mowers at the weekends, and roses.

BOB

(to ALEX)
What do you think?

ALEX

(slowly, looking at it)
If I were a businessman, I'd think it was very beautifully made.

Glance between them. Interruptions: ALVA yelling "Grub up," BILL yelling "Come on, you lot, nosh."

ALEX'S CAR. DRIVING BETWEEN GREENWICH AND HER PLACE THAT NIGHT.

BOB holds the back of ALEX's neck as she drives. She takes it for granted that they are going back to her place. Pause. She suddenly laughs. The music from "Così" is playing over.

BOB

What is it?

ALEX

This weekend *alone* together—we've never seen less of
one another.

BOB

Yuh.

Pause.

BOB

(nicely)
Thanks.

Traffic lights. BOB, hand on car door handle, starts to lean
towards her to kiss her.

BOB

Let me off here, love. I can get a cab.

ALEX

(shocked, concealing it too late)
Aren't you coming home?

BOB kisses her on the neck.

BOB

Got to get me eight hours.

He whistles a taxi from the open window of the car and gets
it to stop. The sort of operation that other people bungle.

ALEX'S STUDIO. SAME NIGHT.

ALEX comes into the room as she left it on Friday night. The spilt ashtray; the newspapers and books on the bed; the remains of the coffee–making in the kitchen.

MONDAY

BOB'S PAD. MONDAY MORNING.

BOB's phone rings over the cut. The title "MONDAY" is on the frame. Circular track around his desk, seen through a jumble of half-finished projects. The phone is ringing from the middle of his desk. Out of focus, we see his heaving body waking up under his Indian blanket. In focus, he leans out of bed and picks up the telephone.

> BOB
> *(on telephone, very sleepy to start with)*
> No, I was just up working till very late . . . Oh, shit.
> But I thought they'd made up their minds about it . . .
> Completely caput, or are they still interested? . . . Well,
> screw it, we'll write it off. What happened about the . . .
> *(picking up pace)*
> Would we get a better deal in Dallas? . . . Well, all
> right, see you.

He puts the receiver down and shoves a pillow over his head to shut out the light.

ALEX'S PARENTS' DINING ROOM. MONDAY NIGHT.

ALEX is halfway through dinner with her PARENTS, who sit at either end of a long walnut table. There is a DOG half-visible at her feet.

MR. and MRS. GREVILLE are inconspicuously upper class. MRS. GREVILLE is wearing an old cardigan over a crepe dress. A MAID comes in and goes first to MRS. GREVILLE with a pudding dish nearly empty.

> ALEX
>
> Second helps.

Glance of family code between herself and her FATHER. MRS. GREVILLE refuses. The MAID goes to ALEX, who takes half of what's left of the pudding. MR. GREVILLE takes practically nothing. The telephone outside rings.

> MR. GREVILLE
>
> That'll be New York again.

MR. GREVILLE goes out. ALEX looks at his remnant of pudding.

> MRS. GREVILLE
>
> *(to ALEX)*
>
> We might as well have some port together, then, as there aren't any men to leave to it.

MR. GREVILLE'S STUDY. MONDAY NIGHT.

Telephone ringing.

MR. GREVILLE is on the telephone to New York.

On his right is a tickertape machine carrying share and commodity prices: tin, gold, lead, copper, sugar, pepper from all over the world.

On his left is a comptometer for working out yields.

ALEX comes in with coffee and sugar on a silver tray. She tries to attract his attention.

MR. GREVILLE shoos her away, continuing his conversation.

GREVILLE DINING ROOM. MONDAY NIGHT.

MRS. GREVILLE is at the far end of the dining room.

A MAID takes away the pudding plates.

ALEX comes in.

> ALEX
> What's all the stuff to Wall Street about?

> MRS. GREVILLE
> Bank rate.

ALEX makes a tired sound.

> MRS. GREVILLE
> No, he's in fine form.
> *(grinning to herself)*
> I haven't seen him so spry since the General Strike.

ALEX

When he was a smart undergraduate, strike-break-
ing.

MRS. GREVILLE

Before you were born. Should you talk about what
you don't know about?

ALEX

O.K. But you agreed with him, yes?

MRS. GREVILLE

I didn't, as it happened. But we were very young. I
didn't think it would matter.

ALEX

Well, it hasn't mattered, has it?
(sharp)
The marriage has lasted.
(long silence)

SERVANT comes in with a silver tray of coffee and a science-
fiction book on the tray. She puts it in front of MRS. GRE-
VILLE.

ALEX

I wish you didn't have David to dine here.

MRS. GREVILLE

He wants you back, you know.

ALEX

(shakes head)
Please.

MRS. GREVILLE

Daddy and I are fond of him.

ALEX

Look, I don't want to talk about it.

MRS. GREVILLE

He feels very bitterly about your having taken the books.

ALEX

They were mine. They were all I took.

MRS. GREVILLE

They leave gaps, he says.

ALEX

Oh Jesus. Does being married ever come down to anything but property, ever?

MRS. GREVILLE

Sometimes.
(she looks at the book she would like to be reading)

ALEX looks at her. Sympathy. That sounded sad.

ALEX

What's the book tonight?
(friendly. Quite tender)
Town Planning in 1580?

MRS. GREVILLE holds up a pulp science-fiction book.

> ALEX
>
> Good lord.

> MRS. GREVILLE
>
> I know it looks lurid, but it's rather interesting.

> ALEX
>
> No, I didn't mean that.
> *(pause)*
> You see too little of people.

> MRS. GREVILLE
>
> Enough.

> ALEX
>
> I mean too little of Daddy.

MRS. GREVILLE makes a movement brushing the idea away.

> MRS. GREVILLE
>
> Well, it's not much use to start wanting things of him.
> *(pause)*
> Though I'm not always very good at stopping myself.

> ALEX
>
> *(looking at her carefully)*
> What? *You?*

MRS. GREVILLE looks away. The telephone outside goes again.
MRS. GREVILLE pours herself more coffee.

ALEX

Well, I wish you didn't have to put up with it. But why do you?

A telephone rings again.

ALEX

The other line, naturally.

MRS. GREVILLE

He's busy. It's a heavy week.

ALEX

Oh, stop protecting him. It's *always* a heavy week.

MRS. GREVILLE

You complain about your father. Perhaps you're complaining about whoever it is you see.

ALEX plays with the RETRIEVER under the table with her feet.

MRS. GREVILLE

Are you in trouble?

ALEX shrugs.

MRS. GREVILLE

Who *are* you seeing now?

ALEX

(gets up)
Same person. On and off.

87

                    MRS. GREVILLE
On and off. You're not giving it a chance.

                         ALEX
I can't see why having an affair with someone on and
off is any worse than being married for a course or two
at mealtimes.
     (pause)

MRS. GREVILLE gets up and goes to the sideboard. She finds
some dinner mints.

                    MRS. GREVILLE
What sort of man is he?

                         ALEX
I don't think you'd like his haircut.

                    MRS. GREVILLE
Is he a hippie? But I *like* hippies.
     (to herself)
They hate business and competitiveness. I think that's
what always attracted me to them.

                         ALEX
     (rudely)
What, you?
     (pause)
I'm sorry. I'm sorry. I'm sorry.

MRS. GREVILLE stands near her daughter and hands her a
mint.

MRS. GREVILLE

Darling, you keep throwing in your hand because you
haven't got the whole thing.
(pause)
There *is* no whole thing. One has to make it work.

Close-up on ALEX's face. Startled and moved. Waiting to
hear the rest. MRS. GREVILLE hesitates and then goes on. An
offering.

MRS. GREVILLE

What you don't know is that there was a time when I
left him. We had different opinions about everything.
Everything seemed impossible.

ALEX

When?

MRS. GREVILLE

You were three. He left me alone. It was good of him.
(pause)
But I was mad not to know how much I was going to
miss him.

MRS. GREVILLE moves to the door. The RETRIEVER gets up and
follows her and then pads out, preceding her. She pauses
with her hand on the handle and then looks back at ALEX.

MRS. GREVILLE

You think it's nothing, but it's not nothing.

ALEX watches her MOTHER leave. Shot shows MRS. GREVILLE
wavering at her HUSBAND's door and then leaving it, hearing

him on the telephone. She is used to that particular disappointment by now. She goes down a long corridor. Sound of adding machine over.

GREVILLE BLOCK OF FLATS. NIGHT.

ALEX clangs shut the doors of the lift and walks down the long ground-floor passage.

ALEX DRIVING HOME AT NIGHT.

Briefly recap section of ALEX gas-mask dream sequence: FATHER bicycling away.

LONDON CRESCENT WHERE BOB LIVES. NIGHT.

ALEX compulsively drives home the long way round so that she can have a look up at BOB's pad. After a while, another shot establishes that DANIEL in his car is doing the same thing. At one point they pass one another. Both have slowed down as they passed the window, but not stopped. They don't notice one another. BOB's pad has a psychedelic window-box. Within, from DANIEL's and ALEX's point-of-view, we see only the horned buffalo head on the white wall.

TUESDAY

ALEX'S STUDIO AND THE ANSWERING SERVICE.

ALEX is at her desk, on the telephone to the ANSWERING SERV-
ICE. "TUESDAY" title on frame.

> ANSWERING SERVICE
> Nothing for you, Miss Greville.

> ALEX
> *(to rob the woman of that small triumph)*
> Well, that's a relief.

> ANSWERING SERVICE
> *(severely)*
> Will you be picking up now?

> ALEX
> No. I'm going to bed. I'm only in if Mr. Elkin rings.
> Tell him to ring twice so I'll know it's him . . .
> *(starts to ring off)*

ANSWERING SERVICE

(silkily)

Miss Greville, have you by any chance tried him at 730-1624? He's often there.

ALEX

I wouldn't want to ring him at that number. It's a doctor, you see.

ANSWERING SERVICE

I know that. It's Dr. Hirsh. Dr. Hirsh also uses this service.

ALEX raises eyebrows.

ALEX

Right.

WEDNESDAY

ALEX'S STUDIO. DAY.

Shot of morning light coming in through Swedish net curtains. "WEDNESDAY" title on shot. The telephone goes, stops, and then goes again. Eventual track round to ALEX in bed, who picks it up.

> ALEX
>
> Hallo, my duck. No, I just haven't had coffee yet . . .

> BOB
>
> *(on telephone)*
> It makes you sound like Lauren Bacall.

> ALEX
>
> That's nice. Are you alone?

> BOB
>
> *(on telephone)*
> Yuh, apart from the toucan.

ALEX'S IMAGINATION SCENE IN HER STUDIO, STRAIGHT ON IN TIME.

ALEX in bed with BOB, continuing conversation, lying very close together.

>
> ALEX
>
> Are we going to see each other tonight?

>
> BOB
>
> I can't darling.
>   *(touches her hair)*

>
> ALEX
>
> I'm going to get my hair cut.

>
> BOB
>
> If you take too much off I'll wallop you.

ALEX'S STUDIO, REALITY, STRAIGHT ON IN TIME.

ALEX now alone on phone.

>
> ALEX
>
> I'll see.

>
> BOB
>
> Is it all right about tonight?

>
> ALEX
>
> Yes, flower, of course it's all right. As always.

BOB

I don't think I can do tomorrow either. I've got to work.

ANSWERING SERVICE.

The WOMAN, with earphones, listens to their conversation.

ALEX'S STUDIO.

ALEX in bed, on telephone alone.

ALEX

Yuh, well, I might not be able to do tomorrow myself.
(she turns over)
That's fine. Maybe the night after.

CLOSE-UP OF ALEX'S FACE IN HAIR-DRESSING MIRROR.

Looking at her wet hair. Scissors snip off a couple of inches neatly on each side of her face and the locks fall to the floor.

Pull back revealing ALEX at the hairdresser's.

TIME-JUMP TO SHOT OF HER UNDER THE DRYER.

The other WOMEN are reading magazines and have their legs up on stools. ALEX has her legs down. Some of the WOMEN have fallen asleep under the dryer, but she is wide awake planning her letter of resignation. She looks in her bag for something to write on and eventually scribbles on the back of a cheque.

ALEX (voice over)

Dear Reggie, I dare say you won't be surprised that I want to quit. I'd like to do it next week. There's no point in going into it, is there? Though I will if you want. I've no stomach for the work, that's all. Sorry about it.

ALEX'S OFFICE.

The usual new enlightened building, like a glass egg-box. PEOPLE come streaming along the corridors, which are scarcely more than aisles, since no one has more than a chin-high glass partition for office walls. PEOPLE still knock on these partitions, as though there were privacy in them, and put their heads round to say "Good night." The office empties. ALEX is left talking to a BUSINESSMAN who is at the end of his tether.

ALEX

You've gone and made a shambles of it, haven't you?
(pause)
This place might be all right if it had any walls.

BUSINESSMAN

It's my age, isn't it? That's all there is to it. If you're near fifty-five, in a properly run business, you go over the hump—

ALEX

(over him)
You shouldn't say "gone over the hump" about yourself.

96

BUSINESSMAN

—and you get the golden handshake or a sherry party, and you can't find another job, and that's that.

ALEX

You'd have got this job we found you if only you hadn't invented that degree. Why did you do it? An *engineering* degree.

BUSINESSMAN

There's no point in going on at me.

ALEX

You'd been accepted and then you had to go and muck it up.

BUSINESSMAN

How am I going to tell my wife?

ALEX

Why come here if you won't let us help you?

BUSINESSMAN

You? It's firms like you that are putting me out to grass. Me and the other fifty-three-year-olds.

ALEX

You told me fifty-five.

BUSINESSMAN

(stubborn)
Fifty-three.

ALEX

(lightly, trying to lift the mood, knowing he's lying)
Hang on to that, then.
(pause. The office overhead lights go off during the last sentence)
Would you have liked to have done engineering?
(pause)

BUSINESSMAN

You're an attractive girl.

ALEX

(fobbing him off)
You've messed this chance up and I don't know if we'll be able to fix another.
(head on hands)
I'm so sorry.
(pause)
They'll take up references.
(she starts to wipe her eyes)

BUSINESSMAN

Don't you start.

ALEX looks at him with great concern. He jousts vaguely with his arms, looking for a target.

She gives him a cigarette.

BUSINESSMAN

(trying to recover)
Well, is there anything you can do or not? Are you an expert or not? I've been behind a desk twice the size

98

of that for thirty years. I've had three secretaries at a time.

ALEX

If it's any comfort to you, I won't be here after next week. I'm packing it in.

BUSINESSMAN

Then who'm I supposed to deal with?

SAME OFFICE SCENE. DARKER OUTSIDE.

Lights have been going off at the far end of the office floor. The last PERSON in shouts "Good night" and waves. The BUSINESSMAN is holding ALEX's hand. They have been drinking whisky. Glasses and a bottle on her desk.

ALEX

(peering at him in her way)
Are you really all right?

BUSINESSMAN

Face-lift's gone, that's what you're seeing.

ALEX lets go of his hand in recoil, regrets that instantly, and watches him, sick for him.

BUSINESSMAN

(truculent)
Didn't you know that?

She gives him a whisky.

BUSINESSMAN

You're the only girl I've ever met who kept booze in her desk. We can get our faces done, you know. For interviews. They told me down the corridor. It lasts two days. They stretch the skin. I surprised myself. I looked forty-two. I didn't go home.

(uneasy)

My wife might have been upset. We're all right, you see. I don't know how to tell her.

ALEX

You mean you haven't told her about the *sack?*

She has pushed her hair back in amazement on this line and then pulled back the skin a little on each side of her eyes.

BUSINESSMAN

(fascinated)

Yes, like that.

He does it himself, just enough to brace the skin, and gives her a grotesque cheered-up grin. His new confidence is rather upsetting.

BUSINESSMAN

How about some dinner?

OFFICE CLOAKROOM.

ALEX is in front of the mirror, not looking at her reflection but at her hands, moving the fingers up and down, stretching the skin, pulling it back from her knuckles to her wrist. Already it makes a difference and she is only thirty-four.

100

DANIEL'S LIBRARY. NIGHT.

DANIEL is having a party. BOB is there and four other MEN. Two of them have young WIVES whom they have brought. There is also a WOMAN of about fifty-five, a White Russian emigrée, who has known DANIEL and BOB a long time. They are playing The Game. Atmosphere of intimacy and a good evening. DANIEL is doing a brilliant rapid mime of "Great Expectations" or "The Greatest Story Ever Told." BOB and the RUSSIAN WOMAN keep guessing right very fast; and BOB, laughing, pours drinks in the middle of guessing, his eyes on DANIEL. The cuts concentrate on DANIEL's hand movements.

ALEX'S STUDIO, SIMULTANEOUS TIME.

Cuts of more hands, as in the last scene. But lovers' hands, this time. The BUSINESSMAN is in bed with ALEX. "Così" continues over this and changes over the next cut into the sound of DANIEL's doorbell.

DANIEL'S HOUSE, STRAIGHT ON IN TIME.

The doorbell has just finished ringing. We pick up the sound of The Game being played. BOB runs cheerfully to the door and opens it, still in the mood of the party. A MAN whom he knows and doesn't much like is standing outside with his head turned round to a row going on in the parked car he has just left. A MARRIED WOMAN is sitting in the front passenger seat, facing forward stonily. The car door is open and she is refusing to get out. Her HUSBAND is walking away from the car down the street, throwing his hands up, speechless. The QUEER FRIEND of the MAN on the doorstep is lounging against the area railings, watching the spectacle.

BOB

What's going on?

MAN ON DOORSTEP

Hi.

WIFE

(shouts at HUSBAND*)*
Journalistic hack.

He continues walking away from her, shouting, without turning.

HUSBAND

You'd better start getting up in the morning.

MAN ON DOORSTEP

(to BOB*)*
They've been going on like this all evening.

WIFE

Where's my manuscript?

HUSBAND

(starts walking back to her, fast)
You bitch. What put that into your head? Have you been at my desk?

MAN ON DOORSTEP

(yells at them)
Oh, do shut up and come in.

WIFE

(not budging, spitting the line out to her HUSBAND*)*
Reporter! Newspaperman!

HUSBAND

I'm going in and you're bloody coming too.

He starts dragging her by the arm. BOB lightly loathes it all. The brawling COUPLE pass him on the doorstep and continue down the passage.

WIFE

I know you took my manuscript.

HUSBAND

It's only a cookery book, for Christ's sake.

WIFE

At least it's a *book*.

HUSBAND

You're intolerable when you're smashed.

MAN'S FRIEND
(*to* BOB *as he passes him*)
It's like a bad bullfight, dear.

Shot of front door closing from the inside.

DANIEL'S PARTY.

The row is still going on. The mood of the first part of the evening has been destroyed. The original GUESTS are trying to keep going, ignoring the fight as much as possible, smiling. Smoking. DANIEL has a bottle of brandy in his hand. BOB is standing near him. They both watch the fighting COUPLE, who are by the fireplace.

WIFE

You'd never have driven here that stupid way if you hadn't had her on your mind.

HUSBAND

Who's "her"?

WIFE

(laughs at him)
Coming through Pelham Crescent!

DANIEL move up to them.

HUSBAND

What's so special about coming through Pelham Crescent?

WIFE

Exactly. That's what I mean. If you hadn't been feeling guilty, you'd have gone along the Fulham Road.

Sarcastic applause from the QUEENS and theatrical yawns.

DANIEL

For Christ's sake, stop it.

He puts his hands on both of them, trying to force a gap. The WOMAN slaps his hand and wheels on him.

WIFE

Daniel, get lost, will you? You don't know a thing about it.

104

QUEENS' VOICES
(from sofa, almost simultaneous)
Oh leave it, dear, leave them be. She *will* do it when
she's pissed.

Shot of DANIEL withdrawing. At a loss, slightly humiliated
and angry.

The row continues as he makes his way to BOB, who has suc-
cessfully closed his ears to the fight and is sitting behind DAN-
IEL's desk opening and shutting drawers.

WIFE
I am *not* pissed.

HUSBAND
And what about *Uncle* Keith, and *Uncle* David, and
Uncle all the rest, then? In front of the children.

WIFE
Don't be pious. What about your *saying* "Uncle" in
front of the children?

HUSBAND
Pelham Crescent is a perfectly normal way to come.

WIFE starts to take off her shirt.

HUSBAND
Oh, Jesus, now she's taking off her shirt. Somebody
stop her.

105

MAN'S FRIEND

She's your wife, darling.

DANIEL

(to BOB, *low voice under fight. Riled)*
What's the matter with *you?*

BOB

Nothing. They're ridiculous, that's all.

BOB finds a stamp and puts it on an envelope that he has taken out of his hip pocket. Unperturbed.

DANIEL

You might help.

HUSBAND

(to room, over)
Once she starts, she doesn't stop.

MAN FROM DOORSTEP

Somebody cart the lovely carcass up to bed. She's pissed.

WIFE

I am *not* pissed, I tell you.
  (she takes off her shirt)

There are yells of ''Shut up'' and responses to the sound of someone having broken a glass. General hubbub. BOB gets up. DANIEL goes quickly after him, grabbing his arm.

STAIRS AND LANDING FROM DANIEL'S LIBRARY.

BOB goes toward stairs, DANIEL follows.

> DANIEL

What's the matter?

> BOB

I'm going.

> DANIEL

For Christ's sake!

> BOB

I've got to.

> DANIEL

Well, go upstairs. I'll get rid of them. I'll come up as soon as I can.

> BOB

Sorry.

> DANIEL

Thanks for the support.

> BOB

They're your friends.

> DANIEL

I don't like them when they're like this any more than you do.

> BOB

Then why see them?

107

DANIEL

I've known them for ten years. I didn't *ask* them tonight. You didn't exactly bang the door.

BOB AND DANIEL ARE NOW ON THE DOORSTEP.

BOB

I said I'm sorry. I'd just rather be on my own.

DANIEL blazes.

DANIEL

That's *fine.*

BOB

I just can't stand people carrying on.

DANIEL

—O.K. Off.

The shot goes with BOB, walking along with his hands in his
pockets. He disappears.

DANIEL'S LIBRARY.

The WIFE is being forcibly dressed by her HUSBAND. Frag-
mented images of the party: struggling arms, a MAN's hands
doing up a WOMAN's shirt buttons, cigarettes stubbed out,
drinks being poured.

DANIEL
(to room, standing at door)
Right. That's enough. Goodnight and fuck off, the
whole lot of you. Get out of my house.

108

BOB'S PAD.

BOB is back and in bed. He tries to sleep.

ALEX'S STUDIO. HALF AN HOUR LATER.

The BUSINESSMAN and ALEX are asleep on ALEX's bed. The telephone rings and they both wake. She goes towards the kitchen to pick it up, having difficulty rousing herself.

Electronic signals. A brief repeat of the earlier electronic image of telephone ringing. The signals and the screen go blank as the ANSWERING SERVICE picks up the call.

ANSWERING SERVICE.

ANSWERING SERVICE WOMAN
Very well. I'll tell her.
(unplugs wires and sits back)

ALEX'S KITCHEN. NIGHT.

She picks up the receiver and says hello.

Dead telephone, as the ANSWERING SERVICE has finished. So she starts to dial the service, her hand cupped over the receiver.

ANSWERING SERVICE. SAME TIME.

ANSWERING SERVICE
Miss Greville, Mr. Elkin rang. I said I thought you were in but not picking up.

ALEX
Charming.

(pause)
Well? What did he say?

ANSWERING SERVICE
(after a pause, with triumph about delaying the message)
He said could he come right away?

The WOMAN goes on knitting. The ANSWERING SERVICE is a little room with a gas ring, kettle, Nescafé, piles of house-keeping magazines. A pleasant WOMAN, wearing boots.

ALEX'S STUDIO. TEN MINUTES LATER.

ALEX in a jumpsuit is tidying the fur rug on the bed and plumping the cushions.

The BUSINESSMAN is straightening his tie and bending down to look at her books on top of her gallery. ALEX runs up the spiral staircase with a brandy for both of them. Then she hears BOB using his key. Through the following scenes she looks amused about her situation, and a bit amused too about the way BOB responds to it.

BOB comes into the studio and ALEX runs down the stairs and gives him a kiss. He suspects at once that they are not alone, from the way she does it perhaps. He takes in the two glasses by the bed and looks up at the gallery. ALEX shouts upstairs.

ALEX
George, come down.

She moves a few steps towards the gallery in his direction while BOB stands stock-still. The BUSINESSMAN comes down rather slowly and she finds herself making an introduction across great distances.

Wide shot of three figures, rather small, as she introduces them.

ALEX

George, this is Bob Elkin—George Harding.

BOB and the BUSINESSMAN shake hands cordially.

BOB

How do you do?

ALEX

(to BOB*)*
Do you want a drink?

BOB goes to the drinks table and starts to mix himself a whisky and soda, using what he regards as his own home with perfect pleasantness but a faint edge. He sees that she hasn't got any soda and goes into the kitchen to rummage in the fridge.

BUSINESSMAN

I must be going.

ALEX

Oh, no. Not yet.

BUSINESSMAN

I must catch my train.

ALEX

Thank you for dinner. Thank you.

She shakes hands with him, then kisses him under BOB's eye from the kitchen.

ALEX

We'll see each other next week.

BUSINESSMAN

Yes.

ALEX

Will you telephone?

The BUSINESSMAN picks up BOB's coat by mistake because it happens to be hiding his own. ALEX sees what he is doing and, almost at the same time, grabs the coat back from him and throws it onto another chair.

ALEX

Sorry.

BUSINESSMAN

You won't be at the office.

ALEX

Next week I will. After that, here.

ALEX follows the BUSINESSMAN to the door.

BUSINESSMAN

(at door)
Goodbye.

ALEX

Thanks again.

BUSINESSMAN

Goodbye.

During this conversation they go out of the front door and down the stairs together.

BOB is left alone for a moment, looking unhappy and despondent. Unreasonably, he knows.

ALEX reappears and bends down to straighten a carpet that the front door has been sticking on, to hide that she is giggling.

BOB is at the fireplace with his back to her. He kicks the grate.

BOB

Does this thing ever work?

ALEX

Should do. It's bloody cold, isn't it?

BOB cranes his neck up the flue. ALEX walks towards the kitchen.

ALEX

I haven't got any logs. I've got a cupboard I can burn.

She reappears after a moment with an armful of old shelves and cardboard boxes, and starts to make a fire in the grate.

ALEX

I am glad you came. It's nice to see you.

BOB

*(picks up his thrown coat from the sofa and rehangs it re-
bukingly over the sofa back)*
It looked as if I was interrupting.

ALEX

You're not miffed, are you?

BOB

Not a bit.
(dignified)
I suppose I thought you'd be alone at this hour.

ALEX

Well, we're alone now.
(pause)
Stop looking desolate.

BOB

You've had your hair cut.

ALEX

Yuh.

BOB

Doesn't look as bad as I thought.

ALEX goes on looking at the fire she has made.

ALEX

It still won't last more than ten minutes. There's some
damp stuff we could get from the roof to stop it burning so fast.

114

ALEX'S ROOF. NIGHT.

The two of them together in the dark on the flat roof. Chimney stacks: wide perspective.

They hunt for bits of sticks and boxes, making a pile to carry down the fire-escape stairs. A jet flies over, making an unnaturally loud noise. ALEX watches the jet zoom away.

> ALEX
>
> Too low, isn't it?

> BOB
>
> Well, I suppose we'll either hear the crash or read the headlines.

ALEX'S STUDIO. NIGHT.

The two of them are lying naked in front of the fire.

THURSDAY

ALEX'S STUDIO. NEXT MORNING.

A bitterly cold dawn. The plants outside the window look grey. BOB and ALEX, naked, go towards the bed from the fireplace where they have just woken up. The title "THURSDAY" is on the shot. There is a terrific racket from a building site nearby. ALEX and BOB lie together in bed. She is on her back with her eyes closed. He is on his side looking at her with half opened eyes. A long beat.

BOB

Who was that guy last night?

ALEX

I told you. His name's George.

BOB

Who is he?

> ALEX
>
> He's a man from the office and he's lost his job and
> I'm trying to find him another one.
>> (*pause.* ALEX *is still flat on her back with her eyes closed*)
>
> Do you mind about him?

> BOB
>
> No.

> ALEX
>> (*turns round to look at him*)
>
> You really *don't* mind that, do you?

Bob shakes his head.

> BOB
>
> No. Not a bit. We're free to do what we want.

> ALEX
>
> Darling.
>> (*she gets up on her elbow and shakes her head, looking*
>> *down at him*)
>
> Look. Other people often do what they don't want to
> do at all.

Pause.

ITALIAN STATE TOURIST OFFICE. DAY.

Tracking past a poster in the window of the Tourist Office,
traffic and passersby reflected, we pick up DANIEL and a
WOMAN CLERK at counter inside. DANIEL, his well-worn map
of Italy spread out on the desk, sketches his route with crosses
and lines as he talks.

DANIEL

. . . then we're going from Bellagio and the Lakes on
to Ravenna—and then—

CLERK

(interrupting him as she slams down brochures)
Bellagio and the Lakes. Mountains. Boat trips.
Views.
(she slams down a brochure for each)
Ravenna. Churches. Hotels. Tours.
(she slams down brochures)

DANIEL

Thank you—and then through down to Tuscany—
here, to Siena.
(makes a cross)

CLERK

(slamming down brochures)
Siena. Churches. Museums. Hotels.

DANIEL

Tell me—I've been told about a very good hotel between Siena and Florence. Somewhere here. Do you
happen to know it?

CLERK

Yes.

DANIEL

Can you recommend it?

CLERK

I'm sorry. We're not allowed to recommend specific hotels. This is a State Tourist Bureau.

DANIEL

But that's ridiculous—since you've been there and know the place.

CLERK

I've given you the official list—

DANIEL

(interrupting)
Look—couldn't for once the Italian State Tourist Bureau be persuaded to break a rule . . .

CLERK

(with pomp)
I'm sorry . . .

DANIEL

Just whisper.
(whispering)
Is it terrible?

CLERK

(relenting, whispers back)
No, it's very good.

T.W.A. TERMINAL. DAY.

BOB goes towards the entrance and inside, passing people. One AMERICAN BUSINESSMAN is saying goodbye to another.

Another AMERICAN is asking about the rate of exchange at the bank counter.

T.W.A. TERMINAL SURGERY.

BOB is with T.W.A. DOCTOR, an elderly and gentle Scotsman.

BOB

I just need a smallpox injection.

DOCTOR

Boost?

BOB

What?

DOCTOR

When was the last?

BOB

When I was born, I should think.

Officialdom with paperwork and serum.

DOCTOR

Going to America?

BOB

Maybe.

DOCTOR

You must go to San Francisco. That's a lovely place.

120

FRIDAY

INTERIOR OF BAR AND RESTAURANT.

The title "FRIDAY" is on the frame.

DANIEL is sitting alone at the bar portion of a restaurant eating nuts and olives and finishing a whisky sour. He is studying the brochures from the Tourist Bureau.

The WAITER comes up to him with a menu and asks him if he wants to order.

DANIEL takes the menu and the WAITER goes off to answer the telephone.

He comes back towards DANIEL.

> **WAITER**
> Dr. Hirsh, Mr. Elkin has just rung and says he's sorry, but he doesn't feel well and won't be joining you.

BOB'S PAD. NIGHT.

DANIEL, with overcoat still on, is shining a torch down BOB's throat.

> DANIEL
>
> Why the hell didn't you say you were ill? Instead of just not turning up as usual?

> BOB
>
> Are you still going on at me about about Wednesday night?

> DANIEL
>
> No, of course not. Say ah. That looks O.K. What have you been eating?

> BOB
>
> I don't think it's that.

> DANIEL
>
> Well, you've got a temperature all right.

> BOB
>
> *(sending him up)*
> Now tell me to take some aspirin.

> DANIEL
>
> *(picking up the note; an old routine between them)*
> Yes, take plenty of aspirin.

> BOB
>
> And fluids.

DANIEL

And fluids.
> (*pause. Change of voice*)

I got the bumph about taking the car to Nice.

BOB shivers.

DANIEL

> (*showing* BOB *a brochure*)

Your temperature's going up.

DANIEL leans over BOB, against the vaccinated arm, and BOB
jumps a mile.

Close-up of DANIEL's face.

BOB

Oh, shit, I'll have to tell you. I had a vaccination yes-
terday. For smallpox.

DANIEL

Why the hell didn't you come to me?

BOB

I just thought—I didn't want—

DANIEL

> (*after a pause*)

That means America.

BOB

I think.
> (*pause*)

Not for long.

DANIEL throws the brochures and some tickets into a waste-paper basket.

> DANIEL
>
> I always knew Italy was a fiction.

BOB gets up and rescues the papers.

> BOB
>
> Hey, don't do that. We'll go when I get back.
> *(pause)*
> I want to, a lot.

> DANIEL
>
> *(glaring. Wretched underneath)*
> It's pointless.

> BOB
>
> Do you want a drink?

> DANIEL
>
> No.

They are both standing. DANIEL turns away and makes himself say the next thing.

> DANIEL
>
> America would be for much longer than you say, wouldn't it?

124

                    BOB

I don't know. I'll have to play it by ear when I get
there.

                  DANIEL

Do you like the people there?

                    BOB

I don't know many. It's a chance.
     (*pause*)
I don't have to go. I could send Tony.

                  DANIEL

Well, that's got to be your choice.

                    BOB
       (*half over him, refusing to accept the responsibility*)
I couldn't ever just piss off, you see.

Cut to close-up of DANIEL's face, raising eyebrows, register-
ing sadly that BOB could almost certainly do just that. And
indeed we have just seen him trying to.

                  DANIEL

Have you told Alex?

                    BOB

No.

                  DANIEL

Why not?

BOB

I don't know what to do. Should I go? What do you think?

DANIEL

I told you, you've got to decide. I can see it might solve a lot of problems for you if you went.
   (pause)
But.

Hold on DANIEL's face looking at BOB.

Cut to BOB's face avoiding that, lighting a cigarette.

SATURDAY

THE INSIDE OF THE FAMILY SYNAGOGUE WITH THE HIRSHES.

The title "SATURDAY" is on the frame.

DANIEL is coming down the aisle. On his way he is greeted by one or two ACQUAINTANCES with nods and smiles.

He reaches the front row of the centre block, occupied by MALE RELATIVES and the men of his immediate family. The relations acknowledge him as he goes by. He reaches an old man, his FATHER, a younger man, his BROTHER, and on the end seat of the row a thirteen-year-old called JONATHAN, the day's Bar Mitzvah.

Affectionate greetings in whispers.

DANIEL
(low voice)
Hello, Father—David—Jonathan.
(to JONATHAN*)*
Good luck.

127

DANIEL glances up at the gallery.

His MOTHER and SISTER-IN-LAW are standing there, looking down. They smile and give little waves of hand. Meanwhile his FATHER gets out a tallis and book from his seat-box and gives them to DANIEL.

Intercut DANIEL's reactions to the ritual, and to his family, including JONATHAN, whose head is still bent to his book, covertly rehearsing his piece. The sense of tribe is strong. It was once a support to DANIEL, up to a point, but he has relinquished most of it, or it has relinquished him.

Sound changes to CANTOR calling up JONATHAN.

DANIEL gives JONATHAN fingers-crossed sign.

Silence.

JONATHAN nervously approaches the dais.

DANIEL, FATHER, BROTHER, SISTER-IN-LAW, MOTHER all rooting for him.

DANIEL'S RECOLLECTION OF THE SAME SYN-AGOGUE IN 1930'S.

The young DANIEL completes the walk begun by JONATHAN.

The young DANIEL is at the desk, before the open scroll. He sings the blessing.

He is flanked by his FATHER on one side, the THIRTIES CAN-TOR and GRANDFATHER on the other.

Before him he sees the expectant CONGREGATION.

—his MOTHER and GRANDMOTHER in the gallery, encouraging—

—his GRANDFATHER and FATHER on either side of him, encouraging—

THIRTIES RABBI

Daniel Hirsh—

Young DANIEL listens.

SYNAGOGUE, IN PRESENT TIME.

DANIEL listening to the RABBI, who is going on with his address to JONATHAN.

Mix to noise of glasses and hubbub of conversation.

THE NAPOLEON ROOM. CAFÉ ROYAL. NIGHT.

Bar Mitzvah party of DANIEL'S FAMILY, their RELATIONS and BUSINESS ASSOCIATES.

DANIEL is weaving his way through the crowd in the direction of JONATHAN. RELATIVES greet him and grasp his hand in passing.

A conjuring COUSIN is doing amateur tricks for some CHILDREN.

Meanwhile, voices over:

WOMAN

Your mother's cousin married a Mayer and John Mayer married Wendy Hillman, so that's how we come to be related—

MAN

We discussed going public but we decided it was too
early—

YOUNG MAN

—not offhand, but come to my office on Monday and
I'll look up the arrangement I made for your brother-
in-law—

YOUNG MAN

My parents were very understanding about it, and of
course I'd never do anything to hurt them—

GIRL

We've just come back from Israel. Daddy planted a
tree—

WOMAN

And this is my other son, Julian. He's studying medicine. He's in his second year and doing very well—

JONATHAN is standing lost in a small group of chattering
ADULTS. DANIEL reaches him and grasps his hand manfully.

DANIEL

Congratulations, Jonathan. You did very well.

JONATHAN

Thank you.

DANIEL'S BROTHER and SISTER-IN-LAW are nearby, talking to
SELBY LOWNDES.

DANIEL

Hello, David.

BROTHER

Dan, can I introduce Selby Lowndes? My new partner.

DANIEL

How do you do.

They shake hands.

FEMALE COUSIN, AUNT SOPHIE, and studious-looking MARK, fourteen, appear.

DANIEL

Ah. Aunt Sophie.

AUNT SOPHIE's face, eager, remembering DANIEL in nappies.

AUNT SOPHIE

You remember your cousin Mark.

DANIEL looks at MARK, to him a total stranger.

DANIEL

Yes, indeed I do. Hello, Mark.

AUNT SOPHIE

Shake hands, Mark. Cousin Daniel knew you when you were only a baby.

They shake hands.

131

COUSIN ELSA bustles up, ready to devour DANIEL.

COUSIN ELSA
Hello, Daniel.

DANIEL
Hello, Elsa.

DANIEL escapes the kiss she is about to give him.

SISTER-IN-LAW
Now don't be fuddy-duddy today, Daniel, will you?
I've put you next to an awfully nice woman. She's
only just got divorced, so will you be very kind to her?
I know you'll get on—

In the banqueting room, CHILDREN are rearranging their
place cards.

DANIEL reaches his FATHER.

DANIEL
Hello, Father. Do you know all these people?

FATHER
No.

DANIEL
Quite a do.

FATHER
Mostly your brother's business associates.

FATHER gives DANIEL a perceptive look.

FATHER

How are you, son?

DANIEL

I'm all right. Fine.

FATHER
(*making do with the answer*)
Good.

DANIEL'S MOTHER bustles up with RABBI.

MOTHER

This is my elder son. Rabbi Eisenberg.

DANIEL

How do you do.

RABBI
(*eagerly*)
You're Lionel, aren't you?

DANIEL

No, I'm Daniel.

RABBI

Of course. You're the one who's doing engineering.

FATHER

No, it's medicine.

RABBI

Sorry, I haven't seen you for so long.

133

SATURDAY

RABBI shakes hands with DANIEL warmly, using two hands.

> RABBI
>
> Nice to see you again.

MOTHER takes RABBI off to meet a foreign RELATIVE, leaving DANIEL with his FATHER.

AUNT ASTRID comes up.

> AUNT ASTRID
>
> Oh, Daniel. How are you? You're looking very spruce.
> *(she intercepts a canapé)*
> Have one of these. Now when are *you* going to give us all a nice surprise?

FATHER's reaction: sympathetic to DANIEL.

> DANIEL
>
> *(expostulating)*
> Aunt Astrid!

> AUNT ASTRID
>
> Still holding out on us—well, it's very selfish of you— you're going to be very lonely—

> DANIEL
>
> I haven't found the right person yet—

ALEX'S STUDIO. SAME TIME.

BOB is hanging a clock for her. ALEX is sitting in a swivel chair. Full-face, gazing at BOB's back view on the gallery stairs.

BOB

Is is straight?

Silence from ALEX; BOB turns round.

ALEX

When are you going?

BOB

In a day or two.

ALEX

(pause)
Why did I have to ask you?

Silence.

BOB

I'll be back. You'll be here. We can ring each other
up.

ALEX

I'm *bound* to be here.

BOB steps back to look at the clock he has hung.

BOB

You shouldn't ever have decided to quit that job. You
need something to occupy that piercing educated
mind. You're at a loose end, that's all.

ALEX

No. That's absolutely not it.

(an edge in her voice that baffles BOB*)*

BOB

I don't get you like this—
(pause)
You could come over. Could you come over?

ALEX swivels her chair away from him.

BOB

(moving clock hands to right time)
Nothing's changed.

ALEX

(furious)
That's bang on right. That's the trouble. *Nothing's*
changed. All this fitting in and shutting up and making do. Me being careful not to ask you about Daniel,
Daniel not getting any answers from you because
you're here, my old mum not making demands for
umpteen years, and my *fucking* office. I don't want us
to live like this. I don't want to live like this any more.
I *can't* come over. *Don't* ring. I won't be here when
you come back. We've got to pack this in and I don't
know what else to say.

BOB

Look. Would it make any difference if we tried to live
together? I don't want to lose you.

ALEX

Hey. Darling. You couldn't do it. Don't even say it—
(tries to light cigarette)

136

Blast! I've got the shakes. I bought your terms, and
they were rotten terms, and I shouldn't have done it.
My fault.

> BOB

You keep asking too much.

> ALEX

For God's sake. Caring about someone a lot? Is that
too much? People with some time to spare for each
other. Is that too much?
> (ALEX *waits until she has stopped crying*)

I've had this business that anything is better than
nothing. There are times when nothing *has* to be better than anything.
> (*pause*)

If you look back on this—which you won't, my darling—you'll say it's got something to do with Daniel.
It hasn't . . .

The phone goes.

BOB doesn't dare move to answer it. He watches ALEX.

ALEX answers.

> ALEX

It's New York for you. Wouldn't you know.

BOB goes to the phone beside her bed and lies down. ALEX
begins to laugh.

> BOB

Put him on.

137

(to ALEX*)*
What's the joke?

ALEX

I was thinking of someone else . . .

BOB

(yelling)
Hi. Shout a bit, we've got a lousy connection.

ALEX

(at the same time, softly, knowing she can't be heard)
. . . of my old mum, actually. You can't hear, and I
love you a lot, and I don't want you to go.

SAVOY BALLROOM. NIGHT.

JONATHAN is on the dais. Glasses and cutlery noises.

JONATHAN

Unaccustomed as I am to public speaking, I want to
thank my mother and father, without whom this
speech would never have been written . . .

Laughter. Banging on tables. Applause.

JONATHAN

—for the love and the care and the devotion they have
given to family life on this occasion when I feel the
great weight of responsibility that lies ahead. I want
to thank all of you for coming here and for the gen-
erous presents you have given me in these trouble-
some times.

"Hear, hear." Banging on the table. Loud laughter. During this speech a WAITER has gone over to DANIEL to tell him that he's wanted on the phone and he leaves.

ANSWERING SERVICE. FOLLOWING TIME.

ANSWERING SERVICE WOMAN
Sorry to drag you away from your party, doctor, but there's an urgent call for you to ring the R.M.O. at St. George's Hospital. That's all . . . no, and Mr. Elkin didn't call . . .

HOSPITAL BASEMENT AND STAIRS. MIDDLE OF NIGHT.

DANIEL with his case is going through the side entrance of St. George's Hospital in Grosvenor Crescent, past wheelchairs and trolleys and central heating pipes.

HOSPITAL WARD. MIDDLE OF NIGHT.

There is a light over SISTER's table. BODIES are turning restlessly in the rows of beds. Towards the end of the ward, screens are drawn round a bed. The distant figure of DANIEL, in a white coat, is in conference. The HOUSE PHYSICIAN is beside him, the SISTER respectfully near.

HOSPITAL CORRIDOR OUTSIDE THE WARD. MIDDLE OF NIGHT.

A dazed, scared COUPLE are sitting in the wide corridor on a bench with their feet together and their hands on one another's. Not demonstrative people. She has a crumpled bag of biscuits beside her and a tray of tea. DANIEL comes towards them from a ward at the other end of the corridor. The scale is immense and the human figure dwarfed. He sits beside the COUPLE and they have tea.

> WOMAN
> *(to* HUSBAND*)*
> Can you fancy a biscuit?

> HUSBAND
> That doctor in the white coat said to us the race is run.
> He doesn't say the same as what you say.
> *(he breaks a biscuit, crying)*
> I remember the phrase because it stuck in my mind.

> DANIEL
> I wouldn't deceive you. I think we might have a chance.

> WOMAN
> He said the race is run, that's what he said.

> DANIEL
> I think that was earlier in the night. She's hanging on.

> WOMAN
> You're not thinking she'd be better gone, doctor, are you?

> DANIEL
> No, I'm not. I'm certainly not.

> WOMAN
> Doctors often say that. They have to, don't they?

DANIEL

(shakes his head)
She might make it, you see. You know that would be best.

WOMAN

If she couldn't move?

Pause.

DANIEL

People can manage on very little.

Pause.

HUSBAND

Listen to him, dear. There's a chance, he's saying.

The WOMAN stares down the corridor for a long time. Overhead lights glimmer at intervals along the great length.

WOMAN

The electricity bills must be terrible.

DANIEL'S HOUSE THAT NIGHT.

DANIEL uses the key and climbs the stairs inside, switching off the lights at each landing as he goes. In his bedroom, he sees BOB in the bed and stands there watching him. Surprised. Happy. Less exhausted. He sits on the edge of the bed and takes off his tie and then his shoes, very quietly. BOB's head is half-buried under a pillow as usual.

DAYDREAM SHOT OF HOSPITAL.

DANIEL imagines that BOB is lying paralysed in a hospital bed. The bed is like the one he has just left at St. George's Hospital; it is also, horribly, his own bed at home. BOB's face is streaming with tears, and nothing will move but his eyes as the telephone rings.

DANIEL'S BEDROOM. FIRST LIGHT.

The telephone rings faintly in the hall below. DANIEL, still sitting on the bed, picks up the receiver.

> DANIEL
>
> Yes.
> *(pause)*
> I think you'd better give her pethidine.
> *(pause)*
> Right.

BOB is awake.

DANIEL puts down the phone and goes into the bathroom.

> BOB
>
> It's bloody late. Was the Bar Mitzvah okay?

> DANIEL
>
> I've been at hospital.

> BOB
>
> Will he be all right?

> DANIEL
>
> She. She may just pull through.
> *(lets out a breath)*

142

Aaah. It's much better now you're awake.

Jump cut to BOB putting his arms around DANIEL, who is getting into bed.

> BOB
>
> You take a lot of trouble about your family, don't you?

> DANIEL
>
> Are you in love with Alex?

> BOB
>
> I don't think so, but I can't be sure.

> DANIEL
>
> The truth is I don't want to lose you.

> BOB
>
> I'll be back sometime.

DANIEL holds BOB's face.

The image freezes.

SUNDAY

DANIEL'S CONSULTING ROOM AND GARDEN. DAWN.

"SUNDAY" title on shot.

DANIEL is playing Italian language-records, wearing a polo-necked sweater and grey flannels. He opens the French windows.

He walks out to his pool and crouches down to look at the goldfish. The sound of the recorded voice comes out into the cold garden. Time passes.

DANIEL'S STAIRS. DAWN.

BOB is coming quietly down the stairs in a raincoat. He leaves the front door key on the kitchen table.

DANIEL is still crouched by the pool. He has his head bent and the sight of BOB going out of the house is not visible to him.

STREET OUTSIDE DANIEL'S HOUSE. DAWN.

Long shot of BOB letting himself out of DANIEL's house.

SUNDAY

ANSWERING SERVICE. EARLY MORNING.

ANSWERING SERVICE WOMAN

We'll be sorry, Mr. Elkin. But you'll be back, will
you? Well, I can't say I blame you. The dollar's where
the future is. I'll give that message to Miss Greville,
yes. And to Dr. . . . ? Well, very well.

She unplugs, and smirks a bit and nods to herself, and opens
a packet of fruit pastilles.

BOB'S PAD. SUNDAY MORNING.

He comes downstairs with rubbish and leaves it outside his
front door. A VOICE from the area yells up.

VOICE FROM AREA

Rubbish belongs down here, Mr. Elkin.

He slams the front door behind him and goes away.

THE HODSONS'. SUNDAY MORNING.

ALEX drives up in her car, looking at the HODSON FAMILY having lunch inside the house. DANIEL is with the FAMILY and
PROFESSOR JOHNS.

ALVA

When are you off to Italy?

DANIEL

The twenty-first, God willing.

ALVA

Are you going with Bob?

145

DANIEL

I don't think so.

ALVA makes commiserating sound, checked by BILL.

BILL

We've always thought we should try to be a bit more grown-up ourselves about having holidays on our own. Separately, I mean. Have you ever thought of one of those Scholars' Cruises? Alva nearly went on one.

DANIEL

It isn't what I'd have chosen.

ALVA makes her own married warning gesture to BILL and speaks to DANIEL, meaning what she says, in her own way.

ALVA

I'm terribly sorry.

Sprightly snigger from LUCY. DANIEL looks at them coldly.

DANIEL

No need.

There is a view of the scene from the outside of the house, from ALEX's point of view, and a long snatch of "Così." DANIEL comes out of the house.

ALEX gets out of her car and sits on the wing of his. They shake hands, absurdly. He sits down in his own driving seat.

146

ALEX

I didn't know you were going to be here. I'm sorry.
You know who I am.

DANIEL

Thank you for not coming in. You must have been
out here a long time.
    (awkward)
Have you had lunch?

ALEX

It's the sort of thing we say, isn't it?
    (pause)
I'm ravenous.
    (pause)
He's all right, is he?

DANIEL

I think so.
    (pause)
This isn't very easy, is it?

She shakes her head.

ALEX

I thought he'd be with you today.

They light cigarettes.

DANIEL

He's gone away, yes?

147

ALEX

I don't know.

DANIEL

It's all right to tell me.

ALEX

I'm sorry. I only had it from the answering service.

They make wry faces at each other. As she goes up the path to the HODSONS', DANIEL raises his voice at her.

DANIEL

You're welcome to them today.

LONDON AIRPORT. SUNDAY AFTERNOON.

BOB buys American magazines and walks to the Pan Am counter.

ALEX'S STUDIO. SUNDAY AFTERNOON.

She comes in and finds an envelope with her name on it facing her on the floor, and a key like the one in her hand wrapped up in a piece of paper with a note:

COULD YOU LOOK AFTER THE TOUCAN FOR A BIT?

The TOUCAN stares at her from the window sill. She stares it out.

DANIEL'S CONSULTING ROOM. SUNDAY AFTERNOON.

DANIEL is in his patients' chair, with his back to camera. His own seat behind the desk is empty because he is managing a Hi-Fi nearer his grasp from this position. The Italian language-record is going.

RECORD

I prefer my scampi without garlic and my wife would like a steak if the meat is first class.

Record repeats phrase in Italian.

RECORD

Preferisco i miei scampi senz' aglio e mia moglie desidera una bistecca purchè la carne sia buonissima.

Pause for the student to repeat the Italian. DANIEL says the phrase, in a shorter time than the record allows. Pause.

Camera starts to move round very slowly. We see DANIEL'S profile.

RECORD

You have used the present tense and the conditional. Now we will repeat the phrases in the past tense as if telling a story. "I said that I preferred my scampi without garlic and my wife would have liked a steak provided that the meat was first class."

The record repeats the phrase in Italian. DANIEL speaks simultaneously with the record.

RECORD AND DANIEL

Ho detto che volevo i miei scampi senz' aglio e mia moglie avrebbe preferito la bistecca se la carne era buonissima.

149

RECORD
Molto bene. Arrivederci.

The gramophone switches itself off. By this time the camera movement has brought us to a view of DANIEL in full face, looking at the book on his knee. It is as if he is the patient now, talking to himself: or to us, it begins to be clear.

DANIEL
We went to hear "Aida" in the open air and it was not first class but we enjoyed the music and the land-scape.

He repeats the phrase in Italian, lifting his head and staring straight at us.

DANIEL
Siamo andati a vedere l'Aida all'aria aperta. Saremmo andati a vedere l'Aida.
　　(pause)
—Bugger the conditional.
　　(pause)
When you're at school and want to quit, people say you're going to hate being out in the world. Well, I didn't believe them and I was right. When I was a kid I couldn't wait to be grown up and they said child-hood was the best time of my life and it wasn't. Now I want his company and people say, what's half a loaf, you're well shot of him; and I say, I know that, I miss him, that's all. They say he'd never have made me happy and I say, I am happy, apart from missing him. You might throw me a pill or two for my cough.
　　(pause)

150

All my life I've been looking for someone courageous
and resourceful, not like myself, and he's not it.
    (pause)
But something. We were something. You've no right
to call me to account.
    (pause)
I've only come about my cough.

He, too, stares us out.

Fade to black.

Full credits.